IRISH FAMILY HISTORY

Marilyn Yurdan

B. T. Batsford Ltd · London

© Marilyn Yurdan
First published 1990

All rights reserved. No part of this publication
may be reproduced, in any form or by any means,
without permission from the Publisher

Typeset by Photosetting, Yeovil
and printed in Great Britain by
Dotesios (Printers) Ltd, Trowbridge, Wilts

Published by B T Batsford Ltd
4 Fitzhardinge Street, London W1H 0AH

A CIP catalogue record for this book is
available from the British Library

ISBN 0 7134 6275 2

346924

Contents

Acknowledgements

Special thanks are due to the National Archives of Ireland for supplying copies of the documents illustrated in the book. I am also grateful to Dr S. C. O'Mahony of Mid-West Archives, Limerick; Michael Tepper of the Genealogical Publishing Co. Inc., Baltimore, Maryland; and Brian Mitchell of the Londonderry Inner City Trust, for their help and advice.

Preface

No one, not even the most experienced genealogist, would claim to have discovered a foolproof method of tracing Irish ancestors. Experts readily acknowledge the fact that the odds are stacked against the researcher's finding out many details about his or her forebears as individuals. This is particularly true of the years prior to the 1830s in view of the disasters which have befallen Irish records – and, indeed, the Irish themselves over the centuries.

One may well be able to trace a family of the name under research, but whether the persons so found will include provable ancestors, or can even be relied on to be the correct family at all, may well remain uncertain. If one is able to locate a Patrick O'Brien, or Kathleen O'Sullivan, there may be no absolute proof that these are the correct ancestors when one takes into account the fact that many Irish names are common enough to make repetition virtually inevitable. In addition, as we will see, Irish surnames still tend to be concentrated in certain provinces, counties, or even towns, and remain recognizably regional to this day.

Sometimes it is only too easy (and understandably so) to pounce on the most convenient specimens which come one's way. This may not present a problem to those who wish to do no more than to compile a list of names, dates and places. The true family historian, however, will often have to be content to confine his or her attentions to how ancestors in Ireland must have lived, loved, worked and died, rather than insisting on identifying them as separate individuals, each with a distinct personality, as can often be achieved with luck and perseverance in British family history research.

The small size and conservative life-style of Irish communities before the 1840s and the subsequent emigration, means that one may be justified in generalizing about how one's own ancestors would have lived, by using details derived from studies of the better-documented communities.

The study of true family history, rather than genealogy which, strictly speaking, concentrates on the compilation of a pedigree created from lists of names and dates, should offer some consolation in that it makes the ancestor into a real, if unnamed, person. Unfortunately, one is still left with the necessity of establishing that ancestor's place of origin as exactly as possible, especially if he subsequently emigrated, and contact has since been lost with any of the family remaining in Ireland.

Obviously, the best way to do this is by questioning older relatives, or elderly family friends who may be less inhibited about telling the truth 'warts and all'. Such enquiries will probably bring to light the county, or at least the province, from which the family came, if not the place itself.

Failing this, an approach to the Irish community nearest to where one lives may yield some clues and suggestions as to the usefulness of old newspapers, diaries or folk-memories which may be available. The Irish memory is generally long, and some elderly person may remember their own parents or grandparents, mentioning something which may provide a clue.

If all else fails, some indication of the frequency and distribution of the surname under research can be obtained by consulting the Mormon Index (see Chapter 5) or other indexes, either in Ireland itself or in the possession of a local family history society.

In the following chapters the author attempts to show some of the pleasures and compensations on offer to those who are willing to try, and thereby learn as much as possible as they do so, not only about their Irish family of long ago, but also something of their present-day relatives in Ireland. It is said that the outsider sees most of the game, and so it is hoped that the Irish will take the suggestions and comments concerning their country and themselves in this book in the spirit of affection and interest in which they were written, and forgive any mistakes and misinterpretations which might have intruded themselves along the way.

Oxford   MY
September 1989

Key Dates in Anglo-Irish History

795 Danish and Norse raids begin. They continue for the next 150 years and result in the settlement of cities such as Cork, Limerick, Waterford, Wexford and Wicklow.

1160s During the 1160s and '70s, the Normans arrive, encouraged by King Henry II.

1340s The Black Death devastates Europe.

1494 Poyning's Law decrees that Irish Parliaments are allowed to meet solely with the consent of the King of England and with his approval of its proposals.

1529 The Reformation Parliament.

1534 The Act of Supremacy passed, by which Henry VIII makes himself Head of the new Church of England.

1535–9 The Dissolution of the Monasteries within the Pale –the area surrounding Dublin which is subject to English law.

1592 Trinity College Dublin founded by Elizabeth I.

1607 The Flight of the Earls of Tyrone and Tyrconnell after an attempt to halt the English conquest of Ulster. They go to the Continent.

1608–11 Ulster planted with Protestants, mainly Scots.

1641 Beginning of the Irish Rebellion and of the English Civil Wars.

1649 Execution of Charles I.

1649–52 Cromwell and the New Model Army arrive in Ireland. The Massacre of Drogheda leads to slaughter, and slavery in the West Indies. Royalist estates seized and the native Irish banished west of the Shannon: 'to Hell or Connaught'. New middle-class Protestant landowners.

1660 Restoration of the Monarchy under Charles II.

1688 The Glorious or Bloodless Revolution removes the Catholic James II from the English throne and replaces him with the Protestant William of Orange.

1690 William III wins the Battle of the Boyne against James's forces. As a consequence, some 14,000 'Wild Geese' join foreign Catholic armies.

1695 The Penal Laws are enforced against Catholics in both England and Ireland. Some landlords turn Protestant, but not the bulk of the Irish population.

1741 A serious famine. An outbreak of secret societies.

1775 The American War of Independence has a profound effect on Irish nationalist thought.

1782 Henry Grattan's Parliament brings legislative independence for Ireland.

1789 The French Revolution gives a further stimulus to Irish discontent.

1795 The Orange Order of Protestants formed.

1798 Theobald Wolfe Tone organizes further rebellion of the United Irishmen.

1801 Union of England and Ireland, chiefly to protect England's 'back door' from invasion by Napoleon. This deals Dublin a severe blow, takes away its status as a seat of government, and damages the Irish economy.

1803 Further rebellion led by Robert Emmett and others.

1823 Catholic Association founded by Daniel O'Connell in order that Catholics may have the right to become Members of Parliament.

1829 Catholic Emancipation achieved. Catholics allowed to take seats at Westminster as the Oath of Allegiance to the Crown discontinued.

1845–51 Exceptionally bad series of famines. Estimated 800,000 deaths from starvation and associated diseases. Some 1,600,000 Irish leave the country.

1851 The Census in England, Wales and Scotland shows about 3% of the population of England and Wales Irish-born and some 7% of that of Scotland.

1861 The Irish Census shows the Church of Ireland to represent only about 10% of the people.

1867 Irish Republican Brotherhood (the Fenians) organize rebellion.

1869 The Church of Ireland is disestablished, thus ending its privileged status.

1875 The rise of Charles Stewart Parnell.

1882 Phoenix Park Murders of Cavendish and Burke.

1886 First Home Rule Bill.

1889	Parnell brought down by O'Shea scandal.
1893	Foundation of the Gaelic League to promote interest in Irish culture. Second Home Rule Bill defeated.
1905	Sinn Fein party founded by Arthur Griffiths.
1912	Third Home Rule Bill passed; threat of revolt by Ulster Unionists.
1916	Easter Uprising and the proclamation of a republic of Ireland.
1919–21	Anglo-Irish War, leading to Partition and the creation of the Irish Free State.
1920	Government of Ireland Act decrees there be two Irish Parliaments.
1922–4	Civil War in Ireland. James Joyce writes *Ulysses* in 1922.
1949	Ireland is declared an independent Republic.
1969	Outbreak of the 'Troubles' in Northern Ireland. British troops go to Ulster. The IRA is revived.
1972	The Catholic Church is placed on an equal footing with, but not superior to, any other church in Ireland.
1973	Ireland joins the European Economic Community.

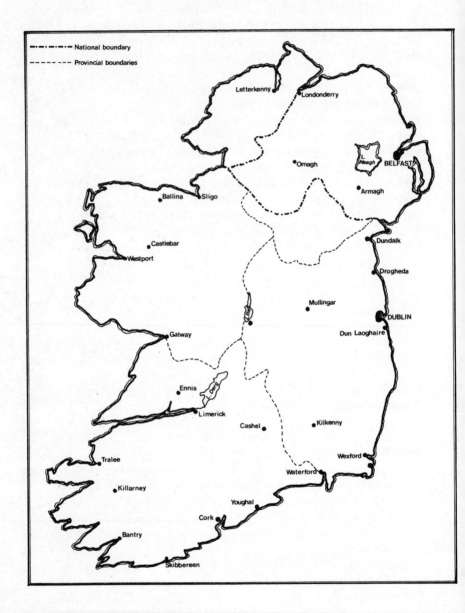

1 *Irish provinces and principal towns*

SETTING THE SCENE

Celtic genealogy in general

So highly did the ancient Celtic chieftains value genealogical knowledge that they employed professional bards and chroniclers to recite their ancestry and compose ballads concerning the exploits of their forebears. The ordinary people, too, were expected to memorize the names of their ancestors.

The Welsh offered a good example of this trend until fairly recently, for it was not until Tudor or Stuart times that they standardized their method of conferring surnames, in order to settle upon a permanent family name which would be handed down from one generation to another. Until this time they had been identified by a string of ancestral names, quite Biblical in their accuracy: Rhys ap Howell ap Llewellyn ap Evan, and so on, 'ap' being the Welsh equivalent of 'Mac' or 'O'. This system survived in remote areas until the nineteenth century, when it was completely superseded by the fixed surname as elsewhere.

The Scots and the Irish, on the other hand, together with the English adopted fixed surnames at an early period, many before the arrival of the Normans.

A link between Scottish and Irish Celts is the concept of the clan or tribe. The Scottish clan system needs little introduction, while the Irish word 'clannad' for family, or group, has been adopted by a folk-group popular today in both Britain and Ireland. What is not always realized, however, is that members of the same clan, even when bearing its name as their 'surname', are not necessarily all related by blood ties, other families living under the authority of a chieftain being bound to him by marriage, trade, or to obtain his protection.

The words 'Celt' and 'Celtic' are used in this book for convenience, although they are not strictly accurate terms, all Celtic peoples being of mixed origin and lineage. The so-called Celtic areas, therefore, are those where Celtic languages have survived, at least into modern times, regardless of the blood-line of the speakers: namely Ireland, Scotland, Wales, the Isle of Man, Cornwall and Brittany.

Maybe, as Kemal Atatürk suggested when describing the various aspects of 'Turkishness', being Celtic is largely a state of mind, a sense of belonging, caring, and of sharing a similar lifestyle, rather than a matter of actual blood relationships. In *Facts About Ireland* (Irish Department of Foreign Affairs) we are told that over half the population has blood group O, which shows a strong Nordic strain inherited from Viking ancestors, rather than Celtic ones. Furthermore, the large majority has brown hair with only about four per cent having the famous red hair!

Irish surnames

The surnames of Ireland are among the most mixed in origin of any in the British Isles, representing as they do the Gaelic, Anglo-Norman, Norman, Welsh, Norse, Scots and English elements which have combined to make up the Irish nation.

Like the rest of the British surnames, Irish ones can be divided up into four main categories: descriptive or nicknames; those derived from one's father or ancestor; those which stem from the location in which the family once lived; and finally, occupational names.

Today the majority of Irish surnames are fairly easily identifiable as being Irish in origin, even if their bearers are no longer so, although some are not necessarily Irish at all, their origins being either the same as British ones, or their pronunciation being identical but coincidental.

Barrett, for example, would be considered by an Englishman to be a typically British name, found as it is all over the country. In Ireland, though, it might be thought of as a Munster name, being common in Galway. The origin of Barrett is, however, the Anglo-Norman 'barrette' or 'cap' maker.

Many of the Irish surnames which are derived from place-names have been adopted from estates held by the Anglo-Norman nobility in both Ireland and mainland Britain, such as de Mandeville, or Stafford.

The famous 'O', meaning 'grandson of', and 'Mac', 'son of', were added to the personal or occupational name of the father, or grandfather, and created these surnames at an early period. Thus we find O'Donnell, O'Brien, McHugh, and MacDermot.

During the renaissance of interest in things Irish during the period 1930–60, the 'O's and 'Macs' were reinstated to their former positions after having been discarded during Ireland's short-lived and most unnaturally respectable Victorian era. In addition, at this time, perfectly good 'English' surnames were translated into Irish, so becoming instantly unrecognizable to almost everyone, English or Irish!

An older and more long-lasting trend was the anglicization or translation of Celtic surnames, when for example Goff, or Gough, became Smith. This led to two or more versions of the same name, a peculiarity which is not always immediately apparent to the unwary.

At my convent school were two brothers, Bernard and Oliver O'Reilly. Oliver, though, always called himself Reilly, because he felt it sounded better. If he carries on doing so for the rest of his life, but his brother retains the 'O', and their offspring follow suit, their respective descendants will probably be treated as separate families.

In Ireland, as elsewhere, changes of surname took place owing to differing dialects or accents, plus, naturally enough, fair wear and tear. My mother's family name, Carey, for instance, which is derived from the Gaelic 'O'Ciardha' appears in Co. Kildare as O'Keary, in Tyrone and Galway as MacGhiachra, in Mayo as O'Cerin or Kerin, in Cork as Carr. Worse still, we are spoiled for choice when it comes to the anglicized form of O'Ciardha; you may take your pick from Carew, Crean, Currane, Keary, Kerin, Kerrane, or even MacKeaghry.

Unfortunately it is not possible to authenticate the origins of all Irish surnames because of the loss of records and family and estate papers, not to mention modern alarms and excursions, emigrating and immigrating which has been going on for centuries, and the aforementioned natural changes.

Nevertheless, one is sometimes able to obtain some idea of the areas in which the name under research is widespread today. Surname maps are readily available; Aer Lingus produce one in poster form, and tea-towels with similar maps can be found in most large stores and souvenir shops. This would be something which it would be impossible to do for English and Welsh surnames, and would prove somewhat archaic even for Scottish ones since the breakdown of the clan system. Tell an Irishman that your grandmother's aunt's cousin's surname was Dempsey and he will probably tell you that this is a Dublin surname – what's more, he'll be right.

There is a steady demand for the items on sale which bear the crests of the dozens of families entitled to bear them, and reproductions of which are available in shops all over the country. Apart from the descendants of Irish emigrants, the English are in there too, carefully selecting their O'Neil ties and their MaCormack cuff-links to take back for their friends and neighbours in Aylesbury or Altrincham.

In 1894 the Special Report on Surnames in Ireland was compiled as an appendix to the Twenty-ninth Report of the Registrar General. It was based on those births registered in the year 1890 and gives the distribution and frequency of the hundred most common surnames of the newly-born in that year. Top of the list were:

Murphy (62,000)
Kelly (56,000)
Sullivan (43,000)
Walsh, which, incidentally, means 'foreigner' (42,000)

It should be noted that there is neither an 'O' nor a 'Mac' in the top four. Some surnames were shown to be distributed fairly evenly all over Ireland, but others were listed under one province, or even in a single county.

As a study of the distribution of surnames at a given moment in history the Report is able to show trends in population movement, and the effects of the Famine half a century previously, as well as of the developing road and rail network and increasing urbanization. As a family history source, however, some care is needed in its interpretation.

Firstly, it must be remembered that, where fewer than five births were registered in 1890 of individuals bearing a particular surname, that name will not have been included in the Report. This means that, while some 2,500 names do appear, many, many others just as Irish, and probably as ancient, would have been excluded merely on the grounds that not enough of them happened to procreate in 1889/90. Secondly, it was taken from all the births actually registered in Ireland, and can take no account of those which were not actually recorded, or children born to Irish parents not living in the country at this time.

Genealogical geography

Before embarking on family history research it is advisable to familiarize oneself with Irish administrative divisions, some of which have no exact British equivalents. These units are given in decreasing order of size. The 32 Irish Counties are divided between the four provinces thus:

Connacht (or
  Connaught)
Galway
Leitrim
Mayo
Roscommon
Sligo

Leinster
Carlow
Co. Dublin
Kildare
Kilkenny
Leix (formerly
    Queen's
    County)
Longford
Louth
Meath
Offaly (King's
    County)
Westmeath
Wexford
Wicklow

Ulster
Antrim
Armagh
Derry
Down
Fermanagh
Tyrone
Cavan
Donegal
Monaghan

Even at this early stage we run into problems. One should be aware that Counties Cavan, Donegal and Monaghan, while part of

5

2 *Irish provinces and counties*

the Irish Republic, remain technically part of Ulster as well. In general, though, certainly in mainland Britain, Ulster is synonymous with 'Northern', or 'British' Ireland. This is doubly incorrect as, firstly, it ignores the fact that Donegal has the most northerly section of all Ireland and, secondly, it ignores the three Ulster counties in the Republic altogether.

To be strictly accurate, therefore, one should refer to British Ulster as the Six Counties: hence the offer heard recently, 'Give us back the Six Counties, and we'll give you back Kilburn!' (Kilburn being a district of London with an above-average proportion of Irish residents).

Next in size to the provinces and counties come the *baronies*, of which there are more than 300. These reflect the divisions of Ireland between the ancient Gaelic-speaking clans and families.

Poor law unions, on the other hand, are relatively modern innovations, having been created under the Poor Law Act of 1838 which laid down that those who enjoyed a certain income were to be responsible for the support and welfare of their poorer neighbours, and taxed accordingly. These unions consisted of multiples of townlands, normally situated within a radius of about ten miles of a market town which acted as a focal point, and where the union poor house was located. Irish unions were very similar to their English counterparts.

Irish *parishes* are of two types. The smaller, or civil parishes (which, by the way, also exist in England) were created to facilitate the compilation of valuations and census returns. Ecclesiastical parishes, as the name suggests, were designated as an aid to Church of Ireland administration, and are normally made up of several civil parishes. In the days when the penal laws were in force, many parishes had a 'mass rock', where lookouts could be posted while the illegal mass was being celebrated in secret.

Townlands are units found in rural areas of the country; they comprise, on an average, some 350 acres, and have no English equivalent.

The subject of Irish genealogical geography is covered in great detail by Brian Mitchell in *A New Genealogical Atlas of Ireland*, published by the Genealogical Publishing Co. Inc., of Baltimore, 1986. The book explores the country's administrative divisions, and shows how a knowledge of their workings will help when researching such important sources of Irish family history as Griffiths' Valuation, diocesan wills and probate records, parish records, marriage licence bonds, and census returns. The *Atlas* includes several maps of each county, variously showing civil parishes, baronies, dioceses, poor-law unions and probate districts. A companion work is the *General Alphabetical Index to the Townlands and Towns, Parishes and Baronies of Ireland, Based on the Census of Ireland for the Year 1851* by the same publisher, as a reissue of the original edition of 1861.

Today, of Ireland's total area of 32,524 square miles, 27,136 belong to the Republic, and in 1981 the population overall was some 5 million. An interesting anomaly is the fact that, according to the Northern Ireland authorities, the Border is 303 miles long, whereas Dublin admits to a mere 280 miles.

The Irish language

The Irish tongue is a Celtic language, a close relative of Scottish Gaelic and Manx, and a more distant one of Welsh, Breton and Cornish. It is not a dialect of English, then, but a proud and ancient language in its own right.

The earliest examples of Irish are to be found in memorial inscriptions written in Ogham, an ancient form of the Latin alphabet; these are believed to date from the fourth century AD.

The development of the Irish language may be divided into four main periods: Old Irish until the Viking invasions of the eighth century; Middle Irish from then until 1250; Early Modern 1250–1650; and Modern from that date onwards. From the sixteenth century an English system of land tenure, and an English-speaking ruling class, emerged.

After Cromwell's invading forces overran the country, Irish went into a severe decline and split into the three principal dialects which are found today, namely those of Ulster, Connacht and Munster. Following the famine years of the 1840s English gained further ground still, but this was an English strongly influenced by the Gaelic in pronunciation, vocabulary, and choice of expression.

It is estimated that at the beginning of the nineteenth century about half the country's population spoke Irish, but after the opening of National Schools where only English was allowed in 1838 further erosion took place and by the Census of 1851 the proportion had dropped to approximately a quarter, of which only a mere 5 per cent or so had no English.

It was not until independence that it became a matter of state policy to reintroduce Irish at an official level, and in 1925 a Gaeltacht Committee was established to study and report back on conditions in the Irish-speaking areas. In 1893 Douglas Hyde had already formed the Gaelic League to try to arrest the continuing decline, but this had been only a partial success, although it did have the effect of awakening a new interest in the language.

Today, Irish is the official language of the Republic, and taught in all its schools. The Roinn na Gaeltacht, or Department of the Gaeltacht, was established in 1956 to encourage a wider usage. The estimated number of native speakers in 1987 was 79,000, according to Bord Fáilte's leaflet on the subject (Bord Fáilte being the Irish Tourist Board). Summer courses for children are available in Ireland and details are available from:

Comdhail Náisiunta na Gaeilge,
86 Sraid Gardnar Iocht,
Báile Átha Cliath,
Éire

Na Gaeltachtaí is the name given to areas in Ireland (and Scotland) where Gaelic is spoken as the mother-tongue, and where the older life-style has, to a larger extent than elsewhere, still managed to keep a toe-hold. The Gaelic-speakers in these areas are almost totally bilingual; these are mainly rural communities with market towns as their focal points, and qualify for special public and local government services.

The principal Gaeltachtaí are in: *Donegal*, the largest in any county, with Radio na Gaeltachta and Irish colleges; *Mayo*, where they are scattered into three divisions; *Galway*, the second largest, but most extensive, which includes Connemara and part of Galway City as well as the famous Aran Islands in Galway Bay, where they claim to reserve English for pigs and dogs, the connection being obvious! In *Kerry* the Gaeltachtaí form part of the Dingle peninsula, and of the Ring of Kerry; while *Co. Cork* has two separate areas, in the north-west and Cape Clear Island, near Baltimore. In *Waterford* the sole surviving area of the East Munster dialect is at Ring, where there is an Irish College; and in *Meath* there are small settlements where Gaelic speakers from the west came in the 1930s, only 35 miles from Dublin itself.

Further information on the Gaeltacht in general may be obtained from an organization founded in 1980 to promote industry and development in these areas:

9

Údarásna Gaeltachta
Ardoifig na Forbacha,
Gaillimh,
Éire.

Irish English

There have been English-speakers in Ireland since about AD 1200; English overtook Norman-French as an everyday language in the fourteenth century, as it did in England, and replaced it for legal purposes later in the Middle Ages.

All modern varieties in Ireland originate from Elizabethan English, based principally on the Northwest Midlands dialects. Most differences in the northern and southern dialects show the influence of the different forms of Gaelic once spoken locally. What we tend to think of as 'Irishisms' are often direct translations of Gaelic words and word order.

In addition, Irish pronunciation shows several survivals from an earlier form of English, saying 'tay' for 'tea', 'aisy' for 'easy', 'daysent' for 'decent' and 'crame' for 'cream'.

When Henry VIII was proclaimed king in the Irish parliament in 1509, the proclamation had to be read out in Irish, only the Earl of Ormonde being able to understand English, so well-integrated were the rest of the Members. By 1600, English was probably on the verge of extinction, even within the Pale, or area around Dublin, colonized and held from an early date by the Anglo-Norman nobility.

New blood was injected, however, by James I and VI's 'plantation' of Ulster in 1609 by Protestant Scots who were able to 'skip about in the bogs as well as any Irishman', as James himself so poetically put it. Present-day Ulster English has been highly influenced by those new arrivals, a tendency further enforced by the English wars and invasions of the same century; Ulster speech shows the dual influence of the English dialects and those of the incoming Scottish settlers and, since those days, has shown itself to be a very conservative form of the language.

Daniel O'Connell, the Liberator, himself a native speaker, would in the 1820s and '30s tell his Irish audiences to start to learn to speak English if they wanted to get on in life. The Irish church was in full agreement, considering Irish vulgar and undignified. Children who did not speak English were punished, even by their

Irish-speaking parents; a similar state of affairs is described with regard to Welsh in Richard Llewellyn's *How Green was my Valley*, where a tiny girl is punished for speaking her native language by a Welsh school-master who speaks an artificial and affected form of English.

Queen Victoria, while staying at Killarney House in County Kerry, complained not only of the excessive heat, but also about the local accent which she described as 'that peculiar shriek', but today most Irish accents are considered attractive by other English-speakers.

Irish population figures

It is probable that after Cromwell's attentions in the middle of the seventeenth century only about half a million actual Irish remained, as opposed to military and administrative personnel and Scottish and English planters.

The eighteenth century saw a steady population increase, and Dublin developed into an admirable capital, only to decline rapidly after the Union.

At the beginning of the next century, the estimated population was about 5 million, the fertility rate being naturally high, with good, cheap food to be had in the pig and the potato, while many homesteads produced their own vegetables and eggs. Although there were potato famines, and what would have been described elsewhere as poverty, the Irish peasant seems to have been fairly healthy and happy at this time.

The 1841 Census, showing a total of more than 8 million people, led Disraeli to comment that Ireland was then the most densely-populated country in Europe. This figure, though, could be as much as 25% too low, owing to the fact that the enumerators, who were nearly all members of the Royal Irish Constabulary, were neither willing nor able to keep track of those families who had been evicted from their conventional, if basic, accommodation.

In their desperation these unfortunates had taken refuge in caves, burrows, and even 'scalpeens' – holes dug into the earth and topped with a makeshift covering of branches or anything else that was to hand. In 1841 no fewer than 45% of Irish holdings were found to consist of less than 5 acres, and because holdings of under one acre were not included in the Census, hundreds of thousands of people were not taken into account.

11

By the mid-1840s, Ireland was reckoned to have some 8¼ million people, which, for the reasons stated above, could well have been in excess of 9 million. Then came famine.

The first post-famine Census, that taken in 1851, showed a drop in population to about 6½ million. Population commissioners had calculated that, under normal circumstances, the population should have reached at least 9 million by that year. According to official figures, then, Ireland suffered a loss of at least 2½ million, nationwide. Of these, the smallest loss was in Leinster (15.5%) followed by Ulster (16%) then Munster (23.5%) and finally Connacht with a massive 28.6% reduction in its population.

By 1861 the overall decrease had dropped to 11%, but by 1881 it had risen slightly again to 13%. During the decade 1861–71, emigration declined somewhat, only to increase again towards the end of the century.

At the close of the half-century, 1841–91, the heyday of the Victorian era, Ireland's population had dropped from almost one-third of the total of that of the entire British Isles, to a mere eighth. In addition, the density per square mile fell, from 251 in 1841 to 144 in 1891. The overall population of Britain increased by 12% between 1887 (37 million) and 1900 (41½ million) but a decrease of 1¼ million was recorded for Ireland, so that by 1900 the population had dropped to only 4½ million.

As elsewhere in Western Europe a feature of nineteenth-century Irish life was urbanization, in this case towards Dublin and, even more so, towards Belfast with its ever-increasing industrial base of factories, wharves, warehouses and shipyards. Thus the population of Dublin jumped from 232,000 in 1837, to 254,709 in 1891 (with an additional 10,000 in its suburbs) and that of Belfast from 70,000 to 255,896 people during the same period.

Living conditions in Ireland

The state of Ireland in the middle of the nineteenth century has been well-documented, mainly as a result of the tragic series of famines to which the country was subject, culminating in the 1840s.

Much of what we know comes from official reports, but even before the mid-nineteenth century accounts left by foreign travellers show that conditions must have been little short of atrocious – not, to be fair, that the Irish involved seem to have been over-concerned. For example, in 1796 the Chevalier de la Tocnaye describes how

> Half a dozen children, almost naked, were sleeping on a little straw, with a pig, a dog, a cat, two chickens and a duck; I never before saw such a sight. She spread a mat on a chest, the only piece of furniture in the house, and invited me to lie there. [In the morning] the dog came to smell me ... the pig also put up her snout to me and began to grunt, the chickens and the duck began to eat my powder-bag and the children began to laugh. I got up very soon for fear of being devoured myself. I should add that I had no small difficulty in making my hostess accept a shilling.

Later, in 1840, the American author of *The Bible in Ireland* writes:

> ... where a bed might have stood was a huge bank of turf, and a pile of straw for the pigs. There was but one room beside, and the family consisted of some five or six individuals. The cabin door being open, the pigs, geese, ducks, hens and dogs walked in an out at option.... On a naked deal table stood a plate of potatoes and a mug of milk. The potatoes must be eaten from the hand without knife, fork or plate, and the milk taken in sups from the mug.... It must be remembered that a sup of sweet milk among the poor in Ireland is as much a rarity and a luxury as a slice of plum-pudding in a farmhouse in America. [Later:] A cheerful peat fire was burning upon the hearth, the children were snugly covered in each corner, two large pigs walked in and adjusted their nest upon the straw, two or three straggling hens were about the room, which the woman caught, and, raising the broken lid of a chest in one end of the apartment, she put them in.

The writer goes on to note that a double bed was set upon chairs and that the housewife came to sleep next to him, while her husband had two daughters and a son to share his bedding: two bundles of straw spread across sticks, with a woollen covering to it.

Unlike their English counterparts, Irish census returns show an interest in dwelling-places. The 1841 Census graded residences into four categories, the lowest being one which included mud cabins without windows and consisted of a single room. It was found that almost 50 per cent of the rural population lived in such places. In general, beds remained a rarity, bedding being simply heaps of rags on the floor. As we have seen, pigs and other livestock shared the family home, their bulk and warmth being no doubt welcome against icy draughts. Outside, most dwellings sported manure heaps which rose up proudly against the doorway.

The source of most of this poverty is generally acknowledged to be the system of land tenure prevalent in Ireland. The landlord's right to his land, throughout Munster, Leinster and Connacht, was deemed to be 'by conquest'. Not surprisingly, this led to bad relations between him and his tenantry, in contrast with both the feudal and the clan systems which acknowledge the obligations of the landlord to his tenants.

Absentee landlords presented a very real problem, not only because they remained wilfully unaware of the villagers' difficulties and hardships, but also due to the fact that the factors and agents in their employ were forced to prove their efficiency by attempting to exact rents, and to make money generally, where so little was to be had. Failing this, their own positions were in jeopardy. The money thus obtained was subsequently spent outside Ireland, and thus did nothing to help the home economy.

There was much abuse in the system of leasing land, which was let, and then re-let, and divided up, in an attempt to make the ground support several families when it was suitable to the upkeep of one only. Tenants were allowed, even encouraged, to get into debt or fall behind with the rent, so that they became subject to the mercy of unscrupulous landowners.

In most of Ulster, however, the system prevalent, that of 'tenant right', produced better conditions. According to this system, compensation was paid for any improvements carried out to the property, unlike elsewhere in Ireland where tenants were considered 'at will' of the landlord, with the result that there was no incentive for them to attempt to better themselves or to improve their holdings, even if they could have afforded to do so. The Belfast area in particular was relatively well off, partly due to that city's rise following the decline of Dublin after the Union with England and Scotland in 1801. Ulster had been 'planted' with both Scottish and English Protestants, who shared the priorities of the professional and ruling classes as well as their religious ideals, thus becoming instantly 'respectable' to London. In addition to these advantages, there were flourishing flax-growing districts in the province. Donegal, however, although historically and geographically part of Ulster, experienced conditions as bad as any found in Ireland.

Famine

Although the notorious famine of the 1840s was the worst to afflict the Irish nation, it was by no means an isolated event. Coupled with a general decline in agricultural conditions and working standards, there were partial or total potato failures in Ireland in 1728, 1739/40, 1770, 1800, 1821/2, and throughout the 1830s and 1840s. In other words, famine was a quite normal occurrence, and was to be found somewhere in the country at almost any given time.

As early as 1729 Jonathan Swift, Dean of St Patrick's Cathedral, Dublin, had seen enough of poverty and starvation to suggest in his 'Modest Proposal' that Irish children who might otherwise starve to death should be fattened up for slaughter, then marketed as roasting joints destined for the dinner-tables of the rich. Of course Swift (who, although a Protestant and very anti-Catholic, was before all else an Irishman) was writing satire, but the idea could have been prompted by events in Portadown, Ulster, where there had been a rebellion in 1641. The accounts of this massacre had been wildly exaggerated, with an estimated total of 12,000 Protestant deaths, and horror stories of widespread rape and of infants being roasted on spits.

By the 1840s famine had become all but inevitable due to the high rate of increase in the population, and the low yield obtainable from the poor land.

Questions an outsider is bound to ask are, firstly, what did the Irish live on before the introduction of the potato from America and, more importantly, why did it play such a vital part in the diet of the entire Irish peasantry?

Ireland was well able to produce plenty of pork, beef, and, above all, dairy produce, for which it is still noted. The drawback, however, was the fact that all this fine-quality produce was promptly exported, usually to England. It was quite usual for home-produced foodstuffs to be more expensive in Dublin than in London, and the Irish agricultural worker was forced to part with whatever his land would yield in order to put the money thus obtained towards the rent due on his holding. Hence the reliance on the cheap, and easily-produced, potato.

The following song, unfortunately undated, was collected on the Kerry-Limerick border. It suggests that any exported food which proved surplus to human requirements went to feed English livestock, while the Irish producers went hungry.

The Yorkshire Pigs

Aroon and aroon! What shall we do? Our name it is fast going
down.
The humour is gone from every man in country and in town
When they gather to a dance, a treat or a prance,
Or to practise a reel or a jig.
Now the ladies can't stay, they must hasten away, for to fatten
those Yorkshire pigs.

When I was a boy, there was credit and joy, and butter and milk
galore.
We had it to share, we didn't spare, for the bonham and the
boar.
While Craythurs keep small, we'll give tay to them all,
Aye, and bread made with raisins and figs.
But I hear them say 'There's the devil to pay!', when it comes
to the Yorkshire pigs.

Up and down and aroon', through Gloshen in June, and from
Brosna to Rathkeale,
There's slips and stores, and well-bred boars to supply the
whole country,
But they'll regret their conduct yet, with their high-heeled shoes
and sprigs,
For the creamery soon, will give cheques in the moon,
For to fatten those Yorkshire pigs.

Oh, my sweet garsoon who toils 'neath the moon, take the sleep
from your weary eyes,
For the men of the mill in Abbeyfeale are building their
factories high,
And here's to the man who lives while he can, and success to the
man who digs.
May we all live to see Old Ireland free, and to hell with the
Yorkshire Pigs!

16

When particularly bad famines hit Ireland in the 1840s, the Poor Law system went to pieces because, when it was established in 1838, the country had been relatively prosperous. No outdoor relief could be given under any circumstances; in other words, anybody in need had to go into the confines of the union poor house.

An Irish union could be three times the size of an English one; an extreme example, Ballina, was responsible for the poor living up to 40 miles away from the town, and these people had to make their way into Ballina or forego their relief, until some change was made in the system. The result, in addition to starvation, was widespread disease, with a corresponding toll of workhouse officials and their families and the parish priests.

As more and more people became unable to work, the land was left untilled and little fishing and animal husbandry was carried out. The country went further and further downhill, as those who were not actually dying were either attempting to gain employment on public works such as road-making or mending, even though most of them were too weak to work at all, or were trying to make arrangements to emigrate. Virtually all that Ireland had in the way of saleable commodities at that time were meal, coffins and passenger-ships.

In July 1847, when the destitution was at its worst, the Temporary Relief Act was passed, whereby handouts were to be received by about 3 million people, although this measure came too late to save many thousands more. In the city of Cork, for example, over 5000 country people were said to be begging in the streets, while nearby at Skibbereen, in the Abbey churchyard, is a memorial to the famine victims of 1846/7. This town was described by an eyewitness as 'one mass of famine, disease and death, the poor sinking rapidly under fever, dysentery and starvation.'

One organization which was outstanding in its attempts to alleviate the suffering was the Society of Friends, or Quakers, and it is to them that we owe some of the most graphic descriptions of the conditions endured. A certain Mr William Bennet, an Englishman, travelled from Dublin via Longford and Ballina into deepest Mayo, and sent back a report to the Central Committee of the Society. The following account, dated January 1846, concerns

17

the area around Belmullet on Mayo's north-west coast and was considered by Mr Bennet to be fairly typical of the condition of the labouring class in mountainous and boggy districts all over Ireland.

Many of the cabins were holes in the bog, covered with a layer of turf, and not distinguishable as human habitations from the surrounding moors, until close down upon them. The bare sod was about the best material of which any of them were constructed. Doorways, not doors, were provided at both sides of the latter, mostly back and front, to take advantage of the way of the wind.

Windows and chimneys, I think, had no existence. A second apartment or partition of any kind was exceedingly rare. Furniture, properly so called, I believe, may be stated at nil . . . we were too much overcome to note specifically, but as far as memory serves, we saw neither bed, chair nor table at all. A chest, a few iron or earthen vessels, a stool or two, the dirty rags and night coverings, formed about the sum total of the best-furnished. Outside many were all but unapproachable from the mud and filth surrounding them; the scene inside is worse, if possible, from the added closeness, darkness and smoke . . . And now language utterly fails me in attempting to depict the state of wretched inmates. . . .

We entered a cabin. Stretched in one dark corner, scarcely visible from the smoke and rags that covered them, were three children huddled together, lying there because they were too weak to rise, pale and ghastly, their little limbs, on removing a portion of the covering, perfectly emaciated, eyes sunk, voice gone and evidently in the last stage of actual starvation. Crouched over the turf embers was another form, wild and all but naked, scarcely human in appearance. It stirred not, nor noticed us. On some straw, soddened upon the ground, moaning piteously, was a shrivelled old woman, imploring us to give her something, baring her limbs partly, to show how the skin hung loose from her bones. . . .

Many [other villagers] were remnants of families. Crowded together in one cabin: orphaned little relatives taken in by the equally destitute, and even [by] strangers – for these poor people are kind to each other even to the end. In one cabin was a sister, just dying, lying beside her little brother, just dead.

I have worse than this to relate, but it is useless to multiply details, and they are, in fact, unfit.

The *Morning Post*, writing on the Famine, confirmed the Quakers' reports, saying, 'The Celt is going, going with a vengeance. Very shortly an Irishman will be as scarce on the banks of the Shannon as an Indian on the banks of Potomac.'

It was not just in the westerly, isolated districts with their absentee landlords, but also in relatively prosperous Ulster, where people had employment in the newer manufacturing industries which were springing up in the province, that the Famine caused such devastation. Traditionally Ulstermen were among the most hardworking, clean and thrifty of all Irishmen, but Armagh was as badly-hit as anywhere in the country. The Ulstermen literally worked themselves to death at their linen-looms, slaving away in their homes; then, when everything else failed, selling or pawning their belongings, their clothes, and even their Bibles, truly a last resort for Presbyterians. An average of 45 people died weekly in Armagh at the worst period, in the poor house alone. The one at Lurgan was forced to close down, having suffered 75 deaths in a single day. As at Skibbereen and elsewhere, not only starvation, but also the attendant dysentery and fever, spread like wildfire.

This unhappy state of affairs continued for four years, from the onset of the potato blight in 1845 until, after heroic efforts on the part of the clergy of all denominations, valiant relief work, the setting-up of committees and associations, and collections from overseas, by 1849 the worst was over.

Collections of clothing and cash arrived from England and Wales and a truly magnificent series of consignments of money, foodstuffs and clothing from the United States. But the disaster was never forgotten, either in Ireland itself or in America, where many Irish had fled and built up sizeable communities of Irish-Americans who had no reason to love England and the English.

Even on the supposedly-prosperous mainland, though, the threat of starvation was by no means unknown, and it must not be imagined that the peasantry there was living off the fat of the land, even if the pigs were. Indeed, the peasant constitution was frequently too undernourished to withstand the diseases waiting to ravage it.

Typhus, cholera and dyphtheria were prevalent in London and the larger cities, as well as in rural slums, as parish registers, inner-city graveyards, and contemporary accounts testify, throughout the nineteenth century. In no other part of the British Isles but Ireland, though, was famine to carry off (either directly or indirectly) several million people, or to cause such a state of bitterness and despair that many more left their homeland for ever, with potentially devastating political consequences.

There is an interesting present-day tailpiece to the story of starvation and the Irish. In the 'Live Aid' appeal arranged by Dubliner Bob Geldof in 1985, the Irish were well ahead of other countries in their contribution of IR£7 million, that is IR£2 per head for every man, woman and child; outstanding generosity from a country that remembers only too well the meaning of famine.

Religion and family history

The Irish Republic is the only part of the British Isles never to have accepted the monarch as the Head of the Church, or to have acknowledged the Anglican church (here in the shape of the Church of Ireland) as the true religion. Southern Ireland remains overwhelmingly Roman Catholic, with no other denomination to rival it. In the Six Counties, however, Catholics represent less than a third of the population; even there, the Church of Ireland is outnumbered by the Presbyterians, a legacy of James I's plantation. Nevertheless, it would be a mistake to underestimate the importance of the Church of Ireland in the history of Ireland. Although its members represent little more than 3% of Irishmen today, in the past it has embraced such famous Irishmen as Goldsmith, Swift, Wellington, Wilde and Shaw.

Even in the south, Protestant sects made a considerable impact on the life of the country by bringing a fresh, critical, approach to their dealings with the professional and landed classes, many of whom came from similar backgrounds; in addition, close cultural and economic ties were forged with the prosperous Protestant nations of northern Europe. While Irish Protestants were therefore socially acceptable, the vast majority of their countrymen declined to question the dictates of Rome, and were consequently seen as little different from medieval peasantry.

It would be a mistake, though, to see Ireland's history of revolt and rebellion as a simple, clearcut Protestant versus Catholic struggle; alignment and re-alignment took place between different denominations and factions, usually owing to economic considerations and pro- or anti-English feelings, as when, for instance, the Protestant middle classes resented the trade restrictions imposed upon them by England. Protestant Irish nationalists include such heroes as Swift, Wolfe Tone, Emmet, O'Connell and Parnell.

Revolts in Ireland were a feature of the reign of Elizabeth, when two distinct Irelands began to evolve; in English eyes, Ireland ranged itself alongside England's traditional enemies, the mighty Catholic powers of France and Spain. So, by its continued loyalty to Rome, Ireland was considered a threat to the English Crown. This fear was only too well confirmed by such events as 'Bloody' Mary Tudor's marriage to Philip of Spain, and the subsequent planting of King's and Queen's Counties (now Leix and Offaly) with Catholic settlers. The burning at the stake of Protestant martyrs, the Spanish Armada, and in Stuart times the Gunpowder and Popish Plots, reinforced this view. The belief that they had a nation of potential traitors on their doorstep goes a long way to explain (if not excuse) the British attitude towards the Irish, often one of callousness bred of mutual fear and distrust.

Still lively in the Irish mind are the atrocities committed during the Commonwealth, and the expulsion of the native Irish beyond the Shannon ('to Hell or Connaught'). These events were recorded by an Oxford historian, Anthony Wood of Merton, who quotes a Captain Gardiner, and his own brother, Thomas, on the 'most terrible assaulting and storming of Tredagh' (Drogheda):

> He told them that 3000 at least, besides some women and children, were, after the assailants had taken part, and afterwards all the towne, put to the sword on the 11th and 12th of September 1649, at which time Sir Arthur Aston the governour had his braines beat out, and his body hack'd and Chop'd to pieces. He told them that when they were to make their way up to the lofts and galleries in the church and up to the tower where the enemy had fled, each of the assailants would take up a child and use it as a buckler of defence, when they ascended the steps, to keep themselves from being shot or brain'd. After they'd kil'd all in the church, they went into the vaults underneath where all the flower and choicest of the women and ladies had hid themselves. One of these, a most hansome virgin, and arrai'd in costly and gorgeous apparel, kneel'd downe to Tho. Wood with teares and prayers to save

her life: and he being strucken with a profound pitie, took her under his arme, went with her out of the church, with intentions to put her over the works and to let her shift for herself; but then a soldier perceiving his intentions, he ran his sword up her belly or fundament. Whereupon Mr Wood seeing her gasping, took away her money, jewells, etc. and flung her downe over the works. . . .

During the reign of the Protestant William III, who had supplanted the Catholic James II on the English throne in 1688, a Penal Code was introduced. This forbade Catholics to: vote in elections; sit in Parliament, or on town corporations; serve on juries; serve in the Army or Navy; teach; enter certain professions or the universities; purchase land; own a horse worth more than £10; or carry a sword. Furthermore, on a Catholic's death, his estate was supposed to be divided up between all of his sons, so that none could inherit large estates, or a fortune. These laws continued in force under Queen Anne and the first two Georges, the first relaxation being in the 1770s, probably as a consequence of the American War of Independence and the French Revolution, in response to which the English authorities tried to engender a spirit of patriotism.

Until the late eighteenth century, then, the average Catholic, at least in theory, was effectively prevented from any sort of advancement, social, economic or educational, even if he were of gentle birth. It is pleasant to record, though, that not all these restrictions were enforced. In order to get round them, some Catholics turned Protestant, or at least went through the motions of doing so, usually in order to inherit property, or to enter a profession which would have otherwise have been closed to them. Supposed converts often boycotted the established Church after their official 'conversion', and would make a show of continuing to attend mass – once their names were safely entered on the Convert Rolls. These rolls are now in the Public Record Office of Ireland, in Dublin.

Sometimes Protestants, objecting to the harshness of the Penal Code, would volunteer to act as trustees for Catholic friends and neighbours, but others, known as 'Protestant discoverers', were encouraged by the government to inform against land-owning Catholics. The discoverer then received the land in question as a reward for sneaking. Fortunately they seem to have been rather thin on the ground, probably because of the risk of a swift and sure retribution, not only at the hands of the Lord!

In 1727 the Test Act was passed, the Test being proven attendance at Church of Ireland services. A limited number of Catholic priests were still permitted and duly registered; any not so recorded who were found practising were put to death or forced to escape into exile. Catholic emancipation was not finally achieved until 1829.

Throughout these tribulations the vast bulk of the Irish population remained solidly Catholic. A religious census, ordered in 1766 by the Irish House of Lords in order to assess liability to pay tithes, was compiled by each incumbent, who listed his parishioners as being either Catholic or Protestant. Many people, who were too poor to be made to contribute, were left off the list as being of no interest to the Church.

The original lists were destroyed in 1922, although copies had already been made for several dioceses.

Many Irish parishes were without either church or clergyman, even in the more sophisticated See of Dublin, the ratio of clergy to parishioners in some cases being less than 1 to 1000.

According to the general census of 1861, a mere 10% of the Irish were members of the Church of Ireland; eight years later the Church was dis-established, that is, it lost the rights and privileges over other churches which it had been accorded under the terms of the Act of Union in 1801.

In 1972 the Roman Catholic Church was declared to be on an equal footing with, but no longer superior to, churches of any other denomination.

The Religious Persuasions of the Irish People (1971)

	Republic	Six Counties
Roman Catholics	93.9%	31.44%
Church of Ireland	3.3%	22.00%
Presbyterians	0.5%	26.70%
Methodists	0.2%	4.70%
Baptists	0.02%	1.10%
Jewish	0.08%	0.06%
Other (inc. No Reply)	2.00%	14.00%
TOTAL POPULATION	2,978,248	1,519,640
Total % of Protestants	4.02%	54.5%

Source: *Facts about Ireland*, Department of Foreign Affairs, 1981

The above table will probably be somewhat surprising to the average Englishman: not the fact that the Republic is over-whelmingly Catholic, of course, but the low representation of the Church of Ireland, and also of Methodists and Baptists, in comparison with his own country.

It is natural for the English to equate Protestant with Anglican, with allowances for the larger Nonconformist denominations, so the high proportion of Presbyterians in Northern Ireland when it might have been assumed that Church of Ireland congregations would dominate, may be worth noting. This is, of course, the legacy of the Scottish planters in Ulster under James I and VI.

It is often stated that it is essential to find out to which denomination an ancestor belonged in order to trace his where-abouts in parish records. This may be true of more recent forebears, perhaps since Civil Registration, but prior to this not too much importance should be attached to what appear to be religious aspects. These may prove superficial, and attendance at Church of Ireland services, and appearing in their registers, mere lip-service to keep within the law.

As we shall see in Chapter 5, 'The Ancestor at Home', Church of Ireland registers contain entries for many non-Anglicans, as it was the only official church until its disestablishment in 1869. Not only were they baptized or married in the Church of Ireland, they

24

also shared the parish churchyard at the end of it – Catholics, Methodists, Presbyterians and Anglicans together, equal at last in death.

Particular Irish problems

Something which needs to be stated at the outset is the undeniable truth that Irish records, whether surviving or lost, have never been of the best quality, and will not stand comparison with those found elsewhere in the British Isles; the reasons for this inferiority are chiefly historical.

Since earliest times Ireland's story has been one of invasions and upheavals, feuds and civil wars, with the resulting mixture of religious beliefs, customs, languages and cultures. Among the problems which arose in the keeping of records were those caused by illiteracy and differences in language, not all those who were literate being necessarily bilingual in English and Irish, with ensuing breakdowns in communication. Due to the tribal system which prevailed in the country from Celtic until comparatively modern times, concentrations of people with the same name, living in the same area, are common, with no sure way of distinguishing between them.

As regards parish records, many people in remote rural districts did not attend church and, indeed, had neither church nor priest to turn to, however devout their intentions. No burial records have ever been considered necessary for Catholic parishes, the only existing ones being kept by the Church of Ireland incumbents. Although Anglican church members represented only about a tenth of the Irish population at most throughout most of its history, Church of Ireland registers, as emphasized above, should not be dismissed as they contain entries for many non-Anglicans.

Unfortunately, those registers which have survived are late in commencing, and often badly-kept, particularly when compared with English ones for the same period. Because of the destruction of so much valuable material when the Irish Public Record Office in Dublin's Four Courts was burned down, when held by anti-Treaty forces during the Irish civil war, even the poorest survivors are now very valuable. This loss always figures largely in any account of Irish family history sources but, as will be shown in the following chapters, many records which one might expect to have been destroyed might never have existed in the first place, due to

25

incompetence, or the late start in record-keeping. This is not to underplay the loss incurred by the destruction of the PRO, but it must be seen in perspective – in particular, it should be remembered that no civil records whatsoever were lost, since they were housed elsewhere at the time.

Although families tended to live in the ancient tribal areas, as has been already stated, the series of famines and the resultant disease and starvation, coupled with the shortage of work of any kind so prevalent in Ireland, drove many thousands of people from their native parishes. Thanks to the high rate of illiteracy and poor communications, these unfortunates often lost touch with their friends and relatives, whether their destination was Dublin, Liverpool or Boston.

In times of famine, thousands lay down and died wherever they happened to be, and were buried wherever practicable, usually hurriedly and in unmarked graves. Those who did manage to emigrate frequently went unrecorded also, owing to the crush at the ports of exit; in fact few officials even attempted to keep records. In addition, vast numbers of emigrants died, either during the voyage itself, or soon after arrival. Unhappily many who survived, in their anxiety to integrate with their new countrymen as quickly as possible, would subsequently reject their own Irishness. This tendency continued until quite recently, for 'ethnic awareness' is a very modern trend.

Thus the most important detail necessary for successful research, a proven place of origin for the family or ancestor in question, is often denied the family historian unless this information has been handed down from generation to generation.

Chances of success

It is by no means unknown for those of us of English, Welsh, or Scottish ancestry to trace at least one branch of our family to Stuart or even Tudor times, the only major obstacle, nationwide, being the Civil Wars and Inter-regnum of the mid-seventeenth century, when most parish registers are defective in some way. As we have already seen, such success is virtually impossible with Irish ancestors, unless they held land or important office, or appear in records in mainland Britain.

Chances of success with Irish research can, of course, vary tremendously depending on the extent and accuracy of any information already known, and the amount of time and effort (money too, in most cases) which the researcher is prepared to invest. Also relevant are the status of the person or family in question and, most importantly, whether or not any entries survive, if indeed they ever existed in the first place. Obviously, even the most experienced genealogist will never be able to trace records which were never compiled.

The outcome will also be dependent on how early the records start and will vary according to the part of Ireland the ancestor came from. As we shall see later, one will be able to trace one's tree further back if an ancestor went out to Australia than if he stayed in Ireland.

I am grateful to Dr S. C. O'Mahony, Archivist of the Mid-West Archives, Limerick, for the following estimates of reasonable expectation for persons doing research in those parts of the country for which he is responsible. He states that for Limerick City the eighteenth century should be a feasible target to reach, possibly as early as 1750, as compared with West Limerick, where one would be lucky to get back as far as 1830. Furthermore, the average Irish family living in the mid-west of the country may perhaps be traced back to 1830, maybe to 1820 in mid-Tipperary.

The success rate is improving gradually with the ever-increasing amount of indexing which is being carried out all over Ireland, and as the results are fed into the computer the necessity of travelling firstly to Dublin, and then on to individual parishes, will decrease.

THE LEAVING OF IRELAND

Three of the principal reasons which induce people to emigrate are poverty, persecution and the desire for self-improvement. If one adds to the total of those who left more or less of their own accord, those persons who were transported or whose occupations took them overseas to live, perhaps for the rest of their lives, the numbers of emigrants leaving Europe between the seventeenth and nineteenth centuries are enormous.

As long ago as the end of the last century, J. C. Hotten started to compile a list of emigrants whose names appear in State Papers. Over the years many more names have come to light and have been included in a much more ambitious work by P. W. Coldham, *The Complete Book of Emigrants 1607–1660*, published in 1987 by the Genealogical Publishing Co. Inc. of Baltimore. The book's sub-title is 'A Comprehensive Listing Compiled from English Public Records of Those Who Took Ship to the Americas for Political, Religious and Economic Reasons, of Those Who Were Deported for Vagrancy, Roguery or Non Conformity and of Those Who Were Sold to Labour in the New Colonies'.

The *Complete Book* is based on Chancery and Exchequer records already used by Hotten, such as licences and examinations, which were an early form of passport control, and the 1624 and 1625 censuses of Virginia. In additon, Mr Coldham has revised and added to them so that they bring the researcher to the Restoration in 1660. He has extracted further information from transportation records, such as those which relate to London's Bridewell prison, and added his own transcription of persons packed off as slaves from Bristol between the years 1654 and 1660, to the plantations of the New World. Other sources drawn upon are court records, port lists and official papers.

Of course, only a small percentage of all those emigrants to North America and Australia was Irish: it was the proportion who left in comparison to the total population of the country which was exceptionally high. Not that this was a new trend, for the Irish have always been noted for their willingness to travel, particularly to mainland Britain. St Patrick himself, as long ago as the fifth century AD, took part in this coming and going, admittedly doing it the opposite way round, for he left England to settle in Ireland. Even today, Irishmen will sometimes define a Scotsman as an Irishman whose ancestors could swim, and those Vikings who were almost certainly the first Europeans to land in North America probably set out from an Irish port such as Limerick.

Over the centuries, the continual feuding and rebellion (the Irish have never been noted for their peaceable attitude, either to each other or to anyone else, although, to their credit, it must be stated that they are one of the few nations which has never sought to invade their neighbours' territory) led to the Gaelic chiefs of old setting off abroad to serve as mercenaries. They took their tribes with them in much the same way that the Scottish chiefs did, and the famous Irish 'Wild Geese' were expatriates who served with the Catholic powers, France in particular, from the late seventeenth to the early twentieth centuries.

The mention of emigration in relation to Ireland immediately calls to mind the unfortunates who fled the Famine of the mid-1840s, with what success we shall see later. In 1848, however, a second wave of emigrants left, mainly for America or England, and these were much superior to those who had gone before them both in education and in social standing. Many of the later arrivals were themselves land-owners who could neither find a purchaser for their property nor afford to run it themselves any longer. It is commonplace to portray nineteenth-century landlords in Ireland as a class of heartless money-grabbers, without taking into account their particular problems or mentioning that the fact that so many were forced to leave was a great loss to the country.

Even when conditions improved, the reports and encouragement of friends and relatives overseas, who had settled down and managed to make a success of their new way of life in an adopted country, tempted many more Irish men and women to join them.

As recently as 1987, the *Irish Post* carried a headline expressing concern over renewed emigration, while an article in *Ireland's Own* magazine stated that 'emigration has again become a problem, and it would be sad to think that all the young people leaving Ireland would be lost completely to their families and friends . . .' unless, one presumes, they have taken out a subscription to the magazine!

Similarly, television documentaries made on all the Common Market member countries and consisting of commentaries by a narrator and interviews with natives of the countries concerned, have shown that EEC entry has done little to help the traditional Irish farming industry, in spite of that having been shaken to its very foundations by modernization. Ireland's economic future appears to rely largely on tourism and on attracting international companies who, it is hoped, will bring desperately needed work to the country, thus helping to prevent its most valuable asset from leaving home.

Preparations before leaving

The first and most important consideration for would-be emigrants was to raise enough money for the fare. The cheapest rate was steerage class, so named from the fact that one travelled in that section of the ship which housed its steering apparatus. For the greater part of the nineteenth century the rate would have been from £3 to £5 per person to North America, and between £15 and £20 to Australia. After the turn of the century, third class travel replaced steerage.

In addition to the passage money, there were extras to pay for, such as travel to the port of embarkation, board and lodging while waiting for the ship to leave – and this could take ten days or so –besides the provisions necessary for the actual crossing, minimum requirements being specified in advance. Once at the port, prospective emigrants were frequently at the mercy of touts and rogues who would offer them accommodation, usually over-priced, and such dubious services as the exchange of hard-earned sterling for forged dollars.

The average weekly wage for a manual worker in England in the 1880s would have been little more than £1 and certainly no more in Ireland, and so emigration often meant the expenditure of every penny of the family savings, the sale of possessions not absolutely necessary for the new life ahead, and, for the more fortunate, the dependence upon cash for a pre-paid passage from friends or family who had gone ahead. Those people who were relatively well off had to make arrangements to sell their land, livestock and surplus goods, no easy matter with all the periods of agricultural depression which were a feature of nineteenth-century rural life in both Ireland and mainland Britain.

At some periods the governments of Australia and Canada would offer financial assistance to persons who, in the eyes of authority, were likely to contribute to the developing ecomony, or whose services were certain to be in demand, such as skilled craftsmen, artisans, farm labourers and domestic servants.

In addition, local institutions and charities, Poor Law unions, trades unions and parishes would all take an interest in financing a respectable family who wished to leave, particularly in respect of the purchase of suitable clothing, footwear and toiletry requisites. References to this outlay can be found in the records of such organizations.

Once the money was raised, a sailing ticket could be purchased from the local agent, often a shop in the nearest market town. Sometimes it was possible to pay half the cost initially, and the remainder on arrival at the port.

Merseyside Maritime Museum's exhibition, 'Emigrants to a New World', has on display a specimen of a Passenger's Contract Ticket, from Liverpool to New York, dated 20 July 1857.

The ticket is made out in two sections, one to be retained by the company of issue, in this case Henry Boyd, 82 Dublin Street, and 27 Waterloo Road, Liverpool, and the name of the ship is the *Harvest Queen*, of 1500 tons. The information it contains is as follows.

Contract: not less than 10 cubic feet of luggage per adult. Passengers to be 'victualled' during the whole voyage 'according to the Dietary Scale prescribed by Law'.

Passage Money: to include Government dues and landing charges – £22 10s.

Persons: Thomas and Agnes Taylor, both aged 50; their daughter Agnes aged 20; their son David aged 18; John Robinson, aged 40 and his wife, Mary, also aged 40; altogether 6 'Souls equal to 6 Statute Adults'.

The passenger's ticket contains all of the above, plus:

Daily Rations (according to the law): to be supplied by the Master of the Ship for Adults. These consisted of:

3 Quarts Water (excluding cooking needs for those items issued ready cooked) 3¼ lb. Bread or Biscuit, not inferior in quality to Navy Biscuit. 1 lb. Wheaten Flour, 1½ lb. Oatmeal, 1¼ lb. Rice, 1½ lb. Peas, 2 lb. Potatoes 1¼ lb. Beef, 1 lb. Pork, 2 oz. Tea, 1 lb. Sugar, 2 oz. Salt, ½ oz. Mustard, ¼ oz. Black or White Pepper ground, one gill of Vinegar.

N.B. Mess Utensils and Bedding to be provided by the Passengers.

The next step was to actually secure a place on board a ship, a procedure which was by no means as straightforward as it sounds, and which usually involved quite a wait.

It is essential to note that those Passenger Lists which were compiled by the British Board of Trade date from only 1890, earlier ones having been destroyed. The most useful survivors are those which were made in the country of arrival, not of departure. The importance of establishing the dates and places of both departure and arrival cannot be exaggerated, for reasons which will become apparent when the sources available in the various countries are examined.

Once on board ship, conditions were always cramped, the accommodation being of the dormitory type, with little heating or lighting, apart from that which was provided by the personal lanterns of the more far-sighted. Sanitary arrangements, where they existed at all, were usually rudimentary, and were largely responsible for the ever-present threat of diseases such as typhus and cholera. Even for the healthy, which the vast majority were not, sea-sickness, not to mention home-sickness, was a constant problem. Terry Coleman's book, *Going to America* (Genealogical Publishing Co. Inc., 1972), gives a graphic description of emigration to America in the nineteenth century and what awaited the new arrivals when they got there.

The Passenger Act of 1852, referred to in the example of a passenger sailing ticket quoted above, was the first to attempt any kind of control over conditions and facilities on board ship, and a second Act in 1855 improved the standards of food, sanitation, medical care, and space available per passenger. Inspectors were appointed to check the state of vessels before they set off.

Prior to this, however, the notorious 'coffin ships' were only too common – over-crowded, and carrying less than the minimum fresh water and foodstuffs for the voyage. The vessels themselves were old, and in a dangerous state of repair before they even left port, and there are records of at least one sinking while still within sight of the Irish coast.

As we have seen, it was the responsibility of the ship's Master to provide daily rations and fresh water for his passengers, the price being included in that of the sailing ticket, but emigrants had to bring along their own bedding and catering equipment, as they usually had to cook their own food, barbecue-style. Apparently, cutlery proved of little interest to some Irish passengers who were observed dispensing with any attempts to use it, and attacking their 'praties' with their fingers, to the disdain or amusement of their English and Scottish fellow-travellers!

Apart from the first Passenger Act, 1852 saw the introduction of emigrant steamships in service to North America, and, by the close of the next decade, steamers had largely replaced sail on the Atlantic crossing. The shipping companies set up a network of representatives, and began to offer package deals, with conditions much improved on pre-Act days.

Under sail the crossing had taken between 5 and 12 weeks to North America, depending, naturally, on weather conditions and destination, whereas in steamers it took only 7 to 10 days. The 13,000 or more miles to Australia, which were largely covered by sailing-ships until steam became general on that run in the 1880s, took between 10 and 17 weeks.

Once safely disembarked, those who had survived the crossing had another ordeal to face in the form of examinations and interviews in the port of arrival; after 1892, New York's Ellis Island became particularly notorious. There was a medical examination, often conducted none too gently, and sometimes resulting in a suspect being detained in quarantine.

Incidentally, the Ellis Island Commission now has a project in hand which aims to list every immigrant who ever arrived there, from 1820 onwards.

After all the hardship and expense involved, intending immigrants could still be returned to their native country if they were considered diseased, or likely to become a burden on their new country. Some 20% of arrivals were investigated, and perhaps 2% actually deported.

Very few immigrants had secure jobs to go to unless they were lucky or prudent enough to have obtained one with relatives or countrymen before they left the Old World. The Atlantic crossing was for the majority a mere foretaste of what lay in store for them – usually another journey into the interior in search of a decent standard of living; this, in most cases, took long years to achieve.

Emigration to the United States of America

American ancestors are by popular tradition divided into two categories, Colonists and Immigrants. The former settled before the Declaration of Independence on 4 July 1776 and, by doing so, qualified for a place in the Blue Book of well-known persons, as Sons of the American Revolution, or Colonial Dames.

Immigrants, on the other hand, were later arrivals who had not had the foresight to emigrate in time to become Sons or Dames, thus becoming a source of regret for their more snobbishly-minded descendants.

Dr Marcus Lee Hansen, who points out these distinctions in his book *The Immigrant in American History* (Harper Torchbooks, New York 1964) goes on to defend the late-comers. He states, somewhat quaintly, that everybody's newly-Americanized forebears were 'all Colonists, all emigrants. And all were engaged in providing America with ancestors.'

The Irish, however, were certainly not late arrivals on the American scene. The Declaration of Independence itself was signed by several men of Irish extraction, which shows that by 1776 certain Irish families had become well enough respected in the New World to be in a position to represent their new country in such an important way.

Even before this, Cork was able to boast two early and world-famous exports, one, it must be admitted, English, the other Scots. The former was William Penn, the latter Alexander Selkirk, who set out from Kinsale in 1703 on board the *Cinque Ports*, to become marooned on the Pacific island of Juan Fernandez, off South America. Selkirk was to win fame as the prototype of Robinson Crusoe.

The emigration rate from Co. Kerry to America was very high, notable Kerrymen being Jesse James's family who settled in Missouri; there is a Jesse James tavern at Asdee. Still on a Western theme, William Cody, father of Buffalo Bill, came from Wexford City which, incidentally, is said to have the world's smallest parish, St Doologue's, all 3 acres of it. Co. Wexford has the J. F. Kennedy Park near Dunganstown, where there are still Kennedys, and whence JFK's great-grandfather left to found the American clan.

Ballyporeen, in Tipperary, produced a certain Michael Reagan, baptised there in 1829, who lived in a cabin where the graveyard is today. This same Michael was destined to become the great-grandfather of Ronald, who visited Ballyporeen in 1984. The Ronald Reagan Lounge now contains souvenirs of the visit, on sale to the public, including copies of the family tree, while the Ronald Reagan Museum opened in 1985.

Even the White House itself was designed by an Irishman, James Hoban, who was born near Callan, Co. Kilkenny, in 1762.

Not to be outdone, Ulster can boast of no less than ten United States Presidents, including Andrew Jackson (Antrim), Ulysses S. Grant (Tyrone) and Woodrow Wilson, whose ancestral farm near Strabane is still occupied by Wilsons who are willing to show visitors round. Derrymen, too, were Davy Crockett's parents and Edgar Allan Poe's grandfather. The grandfather of Henry James, who left Co. Cavan in 1789, came, like Paddy Reilly, from Ballyjamesduff. The Northern Ireland Tourist Board in Belfast offers a map showing the Ulster-American Heritage Trail.

A valuable publication, *Irish Passenger Lists 1847–1871. Lists of Passengers Sailing from Londonderry to America on Ships of the J. and J. Cooke Line and the McCorkell Line*, has been compiled under the direction of Brian Mitchell of Derry Genealogy Centre, and published by the Genealogical Publishing Co. Inc. in 1988. The majority of persons mentioned left Counties Donegal, Londonderry, or Tyrone, for either New York, Philadelphia, or Quebec. The lists are particularly valuable in that they cover the years of the Great Famine and its consequences. Apart from this, they constitute in themselves something of a rarity as they were drawn up in the country of origin, not of arrival as is normally the case.

Unfortunately, American lists normally only give port of departure, and the emigrant's nationality, with few further clues to his background, but these Derry lists do provide a place of residence in Ireland. The book mentions 27,495 passengers, the vast majority of whom travelled on the J. and J. Cooke Line.

Both the Cooke Line records (1847–67) and those of William McCorkell and Co. (1863–71) give the name, age and address of the passenger, and the name of his ship. The principal difference between the two sets of lists is the fact that the former give the vessel's destination and year of sailing, whereas the latter are basically lists of names of those scheduled to sail from Derry, but booked or 'engaged' in America, and give the date engaged, and the expected date of departure. Both sets of shipping lists are now housed in the Public Record Office of Northern Ireland.

Eamon de Valera, on the other hand, did things in reverse. Born in New York in 1882, he was brought up in Co. Limerick, at Bruree, where his mother had lived before emigrating to America. 'Dev' went on to become Taoiseach on several occasions, and finally President of Ireland from 1959 to 1973.

An interesting relic of emigration to North America is the term 'American Wake' which described a kind of combination of dance and wake. The night before a villager was due to leave for America, all the neighbours would come round to the family home for music and dancing, in a kind attempt to take the family's minds off the loss which they were shortly to suffer.

Emigration to Canada

Perhaps as many as 20% of today's Canadians have Irish blood in them. The main ports of immigrant entry were St John, and Halifax, both in Nova Scotia, and Quebec, although at one time Toronto was known as the 'Belfast of Canada'.

It is in the eastern provinces then, that Irish ancestors should be sought in the first instance, partly due to the fact that these, together with British Columbia in the far west, were the first to be extensively settled, but mainly because of the strong trade and shipping links forged by the beginning of the nineteenth century between the Maritime Provinces, in particular Newfoundland, and the ports of West Cork.

Some aided immigration, mainly thanks to grants of land from the Canadian government, was made possible and taken advantage of by large numbers of immigrants from Cork, who settled in Upper Canada, now known as Ontario.

The Canadian authorities, however, were soon to discover that they had a serious problem on their hands when attempting to deal with the disease and poverty which was invading their country with the influx of wretched immigrants, notably from Ireland.

At Montreal, a hospital and fever sheds were set up where Victoria Bridge and the railway sidings now stand. By the entrance to the bridge is a stone, placed there by workmen employed by Messrs Peto, Brassey and Betts on the construction of the bridge in 1859. It is inscribed to the memory of the 6,000 or so immigrants who died there of ship fever in 1847–8.

Grosse Isle was a quarantine station in the St Lawrence river, 30 miles from Quebec. In the emigrant cemetery there is a memorial, near the spot where lie 'the mortal remains of the 5,294 persons, who, flying from pestilence and famine in Ireland in the year 1847, found in America but a grave.'

Of the more than 100,000 emigrants who left the United Kingdom in 1847, a large proportion of them Irish, more than 21,000 died in Canada on, or shortly after, arrival. Of these, apart from those who died on Grosse Isle, 14,706 died in Quebec, Montreal, Kingston, or Toronto, and a further 1,120 in New Brunswick.

It is to the everlasting credit of the Canadian people that they, themselves an immature nation, have such a wonderful record of welcoming the destitute, and providing a refuge for the diseased and dying.

So, for thousands, their dream of the good life in North America ended in nightmare. A vivid account of the appalling conditions, both on board emigrant ships and in Irish ghettoes, notably in Boston and New York, but also in Montreal, Quebec and Liverpool, in South Wales and on Clydeside, may be found in Cecil Woodham-Smith's *The Great Hunger*.

Emigration to Australia

Throughout 1988, when Australia and Britain were celebrating the Australian Bicentenary, no-one could have remained unaware of the fact that transportation to New South Wales began in 1788. The colony had already been proclaimed as such by George III in 1786, and was quickly adopted as a welcome substitute for the American colonies which had recently declared their independence and, not unnaturally, their unwillingness to continue to act as a dustbin for Britain's undesirables. '

Many of us in the Old World, though, were probably unaware of the legions of soldiers, sailors, prison officers and administrators who were needed to enable a penal colony to exist. In addition, many thousands left Europe of their own accord in order to better themselves.

It is now very fashionable in Australia to be able to claim convict ancestors; apart from the dictates of fashion, such emigrants are much better documented than those who arrived as free men, or as famine refugees, even the colour of convicts' eyes being recorded.

When the last convict ship had unloaded its contents at Sydney in June 1849, the number of transportations to New South Wales alone had already exceeded 90,000. Of the estimated total of 162,000 convicts sent from the British Isles to the whole of Australia, between 1788 and 1868, about 70% were English, but at least 25% Irish; these were among the arrivals between 1791 and 1853. The remaining 5% were Scots. Over a million modern Australians, therefore, are of convict stock, but one must beware of exaggerating the importance of this number, for about 940,000 free emigrants also helped populate the country, so bringing the total convict influx to a mere 17%.

A great deal of transportation took place to Van Diemen's Land (later to become known as Tasmania) as well as to New South Wales. Until December 1825, the island was a dependency of that state, with Sydney as the centre of administration. Nevertheless, the Tasmanian capital, Hobart, is itself well provided with items of interest to family historians, such as files on new arrivals which list ports of embarkation, together with related dates, from both before and after independence from New South Wales.

As regards specifically Irish emigration to Australia, the mid-west of Ireland, including Counties Clare, Limerick, Tipperary and Cork, forms its Australian 'Belt'; indeed queries regarding the Co. Clare come almost exclusively from Australia, although the Tipperary area was the one of greatest Australian emigration, followed by Limerick, North Cork, and Kilkenny, in that order.

Tasmania claims an Ulster-born Prime Minister, Sir James Agnew (in office from 1886) who was born in Ballyclare, while Southern Australia and Victoria claim Lord Dugan.

Back in Dublin, the State Paper Office in the Castle holds details of transportees, including notes on their crimes and sentences. To mark the Bicentenary, the Irish Government presented Australia with the priceless gift, for researchers, of copies of these State Papers.

The 1971 Australian Census showed that, since the Second World War, about 3 million emigrants from 60 countries had settled there. Of these, more than one-third (1,024,000) were from Britain, and about 66,000 from Ireland or of Irish birth. Figures for the year ending in June 1984 showed that, of 69,800 immigrants, about 19.5% came from the United Kingdom and Ireland, so continuing a two-centuries-old tradition.

... and to New Zealand

Although New Zealand's existence had been noted by early travellers, among them Captain Cook, it was not until the 1830s that the country began to be settled with any seriousness. That settlement was largely due to the development of New South Wales, and records of the first New Zealanders are frequently to be found there, because early immigration largely took place via Australia.

It was not until the somewhat controversial Treaty of Waitangi in 1840 that the Maoris ceded sovereignty of their country to the British Crown, and so New Zealand is among the newest of the English-speaking nations.

When organized emigration did get under way, the two counties which provided the most emigrants were Cornwall and Oxfordshire. As elsewhere, such passenger lists as do exist were compiled in the country of disembarkation, not in Britain or Ireland. The first vessels sailed from Glasgow or Plymouth, and it was not until 1859 that they began to leave from Liverpool.

The settlement and culture of New Zealand has not been greatly influenced by Irish arrivals, the majority of colonists being English and Scottish, as the names of their towns and villages suggest.

The Irish in South Africa

It has been estimated that about 40% of the white population of South Africa is British in origin; in addition there are those of mixed British and Dutch ancestry, which brings the total to more than 60%. As the white population of the country numbers about 5 million, at least 3 million people have British blood: needless to say, much of it is of Irish origin.

Civilian emigration to South Africa falls into two categories, private arrivals and assisted passengers. As all these emigrants were classified as British, without specifying of which nationality, the only way in which we can make any sort of differentiation is by assuming that anyone whose place of birth was Ireland, was indeed of Irish blood. Of course this is not completely reliable; there must have been others besides the Duke of Wellington who would have protested that being born in a stable does not make one a horse!

Assisted Immigrants, a handbook published by the Biographical and Genealogical Division of the Human Sciences Research

Council in Pretoria, mentions certain groups of settlers, some of which achieved a certain prominence. In 1819 the British Government introduced the Cape Emigration Scheme in order to settle the eastern frontier of Cape Colony around Clanwilliam, at that time disputed territory. This had the dual aim of increasing the English-speaking population and alleviating the poverty and unemployment rife in Britain, a legacy of the Industrial Revolution and the end of the Napoleonic Wars. Accordingly, all over Britain, parties of 'respectable' persons were made up, and more than 4,000 people left in some 60 of such parties, during 1819 and 1820, of which some 350 were from Ireland.

By this time there was a shortage of young domestic workers and apprentices in South Africa and many youngsters were sent off there, including some girls from Irish workhouses. Unhappily, conditions on board the emigrant ships were less than ideal. Apart from the usual physical discomforts and deprivation, there were complaints about abuse and ill-treatment, until the exodus of young people was suspended.

Details survive of several parties, including four Irish ones. Parker's party left Cork on 12 February 1820, on board the *East India* in the care of one William Parker, a Cork merchant who had assembled about 76 men and their families. The voyage was not a happy one, being plagued by quarrels. The emigrants settled in the Clanwilliam area, about 140 miles north of Cape Town, but most of them were not satisfied with the land allotted to them. The party split up, some moving on to Albany in the Eastern Province, where there were already many settlers.

Another ship to leave Cork on the same day as the *East India* was the *Fanny* with a further three parties on board. The first was Butler's, 15 men with their families under Thomas Butler, a Wicklow man from Baltinglass, and a captain in the Dublin Militia. Butler's party had experiences similar to Parker's and the majority of them also moved to Albany, as did Ingram's party of 27 families, who arrived under John Ingram, another Cork merchant. The third party, Synnot's, consisted of 12 families under Captain Walter Synnot, of Ballywalter, Newton Hamilton, Armagh, who was in the 89th Regiment. They too started off near Clanwilliam, but subsequently most of them moved on to Albany. The Captain himself eventually went back to Ireland, but later re-emigrated to Tasmania.

Forty-six single Irish women on their way to the Cape in 1851 were subjected to very ungentlemanly attentions, which may have terminated in sexual abuse throughout their voyage, from those in authority. This led to a great outcry, and from then on great care was taken in order to ensure that single females were free from molestation.

In 1857, 157 single Irish girls were sent to the Cape as potential wives for the British German Legion, which had been disbanded. None of them was in any way forced into marriage. Many were sent to Grahamstown and took advantage of the good job opportunities there, and in the end, very few did marry German husbands.

Between 1858 and 1862 a number of immigrant ships carrying Irish settlers under the Cape Scheme left Britain, but this came to an end when economic conditions worsened in South Africa. Then came the discovery of diamonds in 1866, closely followed by that of gold, and prospectors from all over the world arrived in the country intent on making their fortunes. These latter, of course, came privately, not under any government scheme. After this, in contrast to the situation in the 1820s, there was a shortage of work rather than workers.

Irish soldiers in South Africa

The Irish had a history of serving with the British Army, many poor and needy men, as in other parts of the British Isles, having joined up and taken the King's shilling. At the opposite end of the social scale the Irish gentry, like their English counterparts, had a tradition of sending their younger sons into the Army as officers.

The first Irish regiments to arrive in South Africa were the 86th Foot (afterwards the Royal Irish Rifles) in 1796, together with the 8th Light Dragoons (the King's Royal Irish Hussars). Before the Boer War, though, little interest was shown in encouraging the Irish to join the South African Armed Forces.

It has been estimated that about 450,000 British soldiers fought in the Boer War (1899–1902) of which perhaps 28,000 were Irish, whose regiments were the Connaught Rangers, the Dublin Fusiliers, the Royal Iniskillin Fusiliers, the Royal Irish Fusiliers, and the Royal Irish Rifles, some of which formed the Irish (5th) Brigade under the Irishman, Major-General Fitzroy Hart.

Those Irishmen who had taken citizenship of either the Orange Free State or the South African Republic (Transvaal) were obliged to serve their new countries. However, many Irishmen sympathized with the Boer cause, were only too eager to fight against the British, and joined up voluntarily.

Major John MacBride from Co. Mayo, of the First Irish Brigade, married the beautiful but extremely anti-British actress Maud Gonne, and returned to Ireland to join the 1916 Easter Rising; he was subsequently executed at Kilmainham for his part in the rebellion. The First Brigade fought at Ladysmith and in many other engagements in which they acquitted themselves bravely; they became known as the 'Wrecker Corps', as their task was to destroy bridges and culverts in the wake of the retreating Boer army. The Brigade was disbanded before the war reached the guerilla stage. Early in 1900 a Second Irish Brigade was formed, but not exclusively of Irishmen, under Col. A. A. Lynch, who ended up as a physician in London. The Second Brigade was disbanded after only a short period of action.

Thus, in the Boer War the Irish were fighting on both sides, and therefore almost certainly fighting each other.

When the Great War broke out in 1914 a South African Irish Regiment was raised to serve in German South-West Africa; it was then disbanded but revived in 1939 as the First South Africa Irish Regiment, fighting in East Africa, and in the Middle East. Today they are now a Citizen Force, part of the South African Defence Force.

MAKING A START WITH RESEARCH

Most people's interest in family history research is triggered off by a particular event or circumstance, although many more would like to start tracing their ancestors but never get around to making a start. The most common incentives are a birth or death in the family, other people's enthusiasm or success, or being given documents or photographs which make the past suddenly come alive.

The first thing to do is to write down all you know. This will probably have to be done over a period of days if not weeks, for, surprisingly enough, you may well be totally unaware of fairly basic information, such as where your parents went to school, but may know something fairly obscure which needs checking. Every family normally has a certain amount of records and documents, photographs, diaries, letters, newscuttings, legends, and gossip.

It is of the greatest importance, from the very start, to distinguish between three categories of information: what you know for sure, what you have always assumed to be correct but have no proof of, and, finally, suspicions and intelligent guesses. When items are to be transferred from one category to another, the source of this information should always be noted. It is only too easy to believe as fact anything which one has heard enough times, especially if it is something in which one wishes to believe.

The importance of working backwards from one's own generation must be realised. Never, for either snobbish, senti-mental, or other reasons, be tempted to select an 'ancestor' and then try to prove descent from him or his immediate family.

Fill in your own personal details in full, then those of your parents and grandparents, not forgetting other relatives who might be of interest at a later date, or whose particulars might provide a clue to something missing from the direct line. At first use your own knowledge of what is correct, only filling in from hearsay later, distinguishing at all times between fact and supposition. Always be prepared to revise what once seemed to be a certainty, for very little can be certain where human beings are concerned.

Pester relatives kindly but firmly, older ones in particular, and do not be put off by laziness or the effort of getting in contact with them. The most interested and helpful of relations could lose their faculties, move away, die, quarrel with your branch of the family, remarry and even emigrate, while you are deciding that you will visit next spring, but that at the moment the days are too short to go all the way up to Newcastle.

Many elderly people give up their own homes to move in with relatives, or into sheltered housing, and this moving time is an extra-dangerous time for family history material, which may well be lost, damaged, or deliberately destroyed. Nothing is more distressing to the historian than the information that a certain item existed until a few months ago, complete with priceless information, only to have been ruthlessly burned. Equally frustrating are the recently lost family portrait photographs, and the surviving ones, sitting pathetically in junk shops, waiting to be re-united with descendants who will never recognize them because none of the photos are labelled.

As well as relatives, do not hesitate to approach long-standing friends of the family. These may be more honest and less inhibited about telling the truth than are your actual relatives; furthermore they may be more interested in what you are trying to do, or simply have a better memory.

When getting in touch with comparative strangers who may or may not know anything about what you are trying to find out, it is a good idea to prepare a set of definite questions, preferably ones to which there are one-word answers. If the questionnaire is returned with some promising answers, one can push ahead with more demanding requests, but if the initial questions are too involved, or the informant has only a little information to impart, he or she may shy away from anything too complicated.

When outside information begins to come in, care must be taken with the findings. With the best of intentions, the elderly could be missing out a generation, or confusing two people with similar names or of like appearance. They may also be over-anxious to help, or not want to admit that they do not know or remember. Even worse, they may tell you any old story just to be rid of your questioning.

Establish if there are any known relatives outside the immediate vicinity in which your family now lives. If so, try to get as much information about them as individuals as you possibly can. Not only will people be flattered that you have bothered to interest yourself in them as people, you may also turn up some relevant facts which could prove of use in future research. Certain items, such as the membership of a trade or profession, or physical or temperamental characteristics, tend to be passed down the generations, and may surface as far away as Canada or New Zealand.

Start writing around, then, enclosing a stamped addressed envelope or International Reply Coupons, as appropriate. Keep the first letter short and your questions as basic as possible, requiring little more from your new contacts than Yes/No/Don't Know/Can Try to Find Out. Do show an interest in them and their families, not just as reference books, and ask if they can put you in touch with any other family members who might be more interested or of greater use in your research.

Having done as much as you can as regards making contacts and issuing lists of questions to fill in the gaps in your knowledge, it is now a suitable time to establish what you have, or hope to have, and what you still need to find out at this stage. It is useful to show this by means of an outline chart, however simple, on which you can see at a glance what you know and what you need to know. In addition to clarifying things in your own mind, it will be valuable to send to anyone who has agreed to help with your research. As well as the chart showing the direct line of descent, a sort of 'curriculum vitae' for each ancestor should be compiled, with the aim of filling in the following details:

Names
Date of Birth and Baptism, with place of both events.
Education and Qualifications, if any.
Marriage: Date; Spouse(s); Place; Minister; Witnesses; Signatures.
Children, with names of their Spouses, where applicable.
Occupations, with dates.
Any Claims to Fame, or Achievements.
Death: Date, Place, and Cause.
Burial: Date and Place.
Will.

Included should be a column showing the source of each item of information. It is unlikely that, at this early stage, you will be able to fill in more than one or two sections for anyone further back then your parents or grandparents, but the sense of achievement when one can do so is very encouraging.

By now you should have some clear idea as to how and where your research is progressing, and it is time to establish the whereabouts of 'officialdom', that is the names and addresses of your local repositories, libraries and local history collections, as well as something about relevant Public or County Record Offices (the latter in England and Wales, only) not to mention Registrar's Offices and family history societies. When the information to hand has been organized as profitably as possible, arrange a visit to the repository or library which will be of most help, not forgetting that it is usually necessary to book in advance, especially if you are going to need to use a microfilm or microfiche reader. It is also sensible to make sure that the sources which you mean to consult are, in fact, held where you believe them to be. It is not uncommon for parish registers, for example, to be out on loan to family history societies, whose members may be making typed transcripts for general use. This time-consuming and exacting task will take months, if not years, to accomplish from beginning to end, and you may be advised to contact the transcriber rather than the custodian.

Try to find out if a written or published pedigree already exists for the name under research. Large libraries and societies hold hundreds of these trees, although they will not vouch for their accuracy. If such a pedigree does exist, obtain a copy for reference, for it would be a great waste of time to duplicate all the time and effort which went into its compilation. However, do not jump to conclusions either way about its relevance to your own particular family. Never assume that they must be the same, even if in different branches; on the other hand, do not be put off by mention of title or coats of arms, for many titled families have slipped down the social scale, died out in all but the most junior branches, or produced illegitimate offshoots which have kept well away from the main branch until there is little or no connection between them.

The definitive work on historic Irish pedigrees, John O'Hart's *Irish Pedigrees* which appeared in Dublin last century, has been reissued as a copy of the 5th edition (1892) by the Genealogical

Publishing Co. Inc., in two volumes. Starting with legendary families from pre-Celtic days, it progresses through the Norman and English occupations, including that of Cromwell, continuing in most cases until the last decades of the nineteenth century, and following the fortunes of some Irish families across the Atlantic. Accounts are given, not only of notable Anglo-Irish families, but also of the French Huguenots, German Palatines and 'planted' Scots. Also listed are Irish mercenaries serving with the Catholic Powers and in the Americas, and 'Wild Geese' and their descendants.

By now you should be aware of which county or counties your ancestors lived in, and joining a family history society will put you in touch with people living in the area, or of similar interests to yourself. It is worthwhile taking out a subscription both to a local society and to a national magazine like the British *Family Tree*. Magazines and journals are only one of the many advantages of joining a society. Even if you have no known connection with the area in which you now live, society members will have a wide assortment of talents and levels of experience, and will be able to put you in touch with someone with the expertise which you require. Societies also run their own libraries and bookstalls, not to mention keeping back copies of their own publications. Work through these journals for mention of your ancestral parish and family, and scan the Members' Interests column for someone doing similar research. If no-one has already advertised, place your own advertisement.

Any self-respecting family history society will be engaged in all manner of compilation and transcription work, and will be in need of volunteers to help. This is particularly true in Ireland where new societies are being formed every year and any type of assistance will be welcome, from transcription to typing, from editing journals and addressing envelopes, to putting on the wellies and going to the local graveyard to copy out the inscriptions before they are lost to the elements for all time.

Helping out is the best way to develop your own research skills, besides being a sociable activity and a service to the community. By starting with something relatively simple, such as a census return, or a later parish register, you will gradually become more and more competent at tackling the more ancient or damaged sources, thus applying the golden rule of beginning with the present and working backwards.

As you gather an increasing amount of information about your forebears, you may well need specialist help to deal with certain aspects of their lives which are puzzling to an outsider. Once again, your local family history society may be able to help, or at least put you in contact with the relevant authorities. This is certainly true of the professions, of the Church, of certain trades and crafts, of the more obscure religious denominations, and of the Armed Services.

For those people who no longer live in Ireland, and are not in close contact with the Irish way of life, history and culture, a certain amount of background reading would not come amiss. At the very least several general histories and economic studies should be consulted, preferably ones written from both angles, or published by the Irish Government departments, or the Tourist Boards. It is also interesting to read accounts of Irish life and history written at different periods, and by travellers from various countries. It is unlikely that the beginner, without any historical training, will be able to make much sense of the heavier works on the subject, and so compilations by various Irish men and women in the public eye – poets, novelists, actors, politicians, personalities – may give more food for thought. Of interest too, are novels which do not consciously seek to instruct, and can be all the more informative for this reason. Many an ancestor will have been like one or more of the characters in Somerville and Ross's *Experiences of an Irish R.M.* (Resident Magistrate), or in the adventures of James Joyce's heroes and heroines.

Works dealing with the actual area from which your family came will prove of the utmost importance, as the following example will show.

Portrait of a parish

Ballynakill (Báile na Cille: the townland of the church) is one of four parishes making up the barony of Ballynahinch in the north of Co. Galway. It is also the subject of a very readable paperback book, *Portrait of a Parish, Ballynakill, Connemara*, produced by the Tully Cross Guild of the Irish Countrywomen's Association, in 1985. For the year 1983–4, the I.C.A. chose as their national theme 'Our Heritage', and this book, with others like it, is the result.

Ballynakill is a typical example of a poor, underprivileged Irish rural parish. It is reasonable to assume, therefore, that the majority of similar parishes, all over the country, might be portrayed with similar thoroughness. The following outline of the book demonstrates the sources available to the local historian, and the use which may be made of them.

Ballynakill was established as a parish in 1585. Following Cromwell's Act of Settlement of Ireland, in 1652, rebel property was liable to confiscation, and some 100,000 persons for execution. The Act empowered the authorities to transport rebel Irishmen, for the most part to the West Indies as slaves. Troublesome Englishmen, notably Parliamentarian soldiers, were treated similarly, indeed some were actually sent to the West Indies for refusing to serve in Ireland. A later Act awarded land to the Army in lieu of pay.

After the Restoration in 1660, rebel land was distributed among Royalists, and the *Portrait* contains a list of principal beneficiaries of profitable land.

A description of the parish as it was in 1684 follows, but little more is recorded from the introduction of the Penal Code under William III, until its lifting in 1829. Soon afterwards both fee-paying and free schools were established in Ballynakill.

The section 'Parish and People', includes surveys for bog reclamation in 1814, family letters, and the details of the founding of a Girls' School in about 1820, by the Kildare Street Society of Dublin, which had been founded 'to promote basic education among the lower classes.' Also mentioned are a series of famines.

In 1839 came the first modern surveys for the overall Ordnance Survey, leading to Sir Richard Griffith's valuations of 1855, the results of which are still useful for rating purposes.

The 1841 Census showed Ballynakill's population as 7,928 (in 1981 it was less than 2,000) made up of 1,440 families occupying 1,421 houses, all but 19 of which were built of mud. The poorest category of accommodation housed 91% of the population, nearly double the Co. Galway average of 53%. The average Ballynakill family had 5 members, the occupations of the males being chiefly agriculture and fishing, those of the women mainly spinning and weaving. Of those parishioners aged five years and over, 88% were illiterate, showing the area to be one of the worst in Ireland in this respect.

1845 brought the onset of the Great Famine, which was to worsen by the following year. Between 1846 and 1848 the Ballynakill district was as badly affected as anywhere in the country. The population dropped from its 1841 total of 7,928 to 4,808 in 1851, an overall loss of 20%, with subsequent depopulation of the townlands. Not surprisingly, there were 'converts' to Protestantism, who wished to qualify for famine relief.

In the autumn of 1846 a relief committee was set up to organize the collection of funds and subscriptions with which to buy desperately needed foodstuffs and equipment, and correspondence was entered into with the Government.

There are notes on Quaker relief work, and a description of the barony of Ballynahinch compiled by various visitors; also letters which passed to and from members of the district's leading families.

The Griffith's Valuation of 1855 for Ballynakill shows a somewhat dismal picture of 73 townlands, and 47,922 statute acres, of which 540 were under water, 75% of the remainder being either mountainous or boggy terrain, with only 25% farm land. The mid-nineteenth century was a period of large estates, big houses and demesnes, absentee landlords, and small farmers. We are given the names of house occupants in the parish in 1855, together with the commonest surnames both then and now, and their frequency. It is interesting to find a good proportion of Scottish, Welsh, and generally British surnames among the traditional Irish ones.

The 1870s showed the effects of increasing support for the Home Rule movement in the area. The section of the book which deals with religion in the nineteenth century mentions conflict between the various Catholic, Church of England and Presbyterian families, and provides a list of parish priests and rectors to date.

Regarding education, there are lists of pupils attending certain schools at set dates; National School roll-books; names of teachers; mention of conditions (bring your own turf to school in the morning); as well as details of the curriculum, which show that Irish was first taught as a set subject in 1904.

The 1880s brought agitation for land reform, here as elsewhere in the British Isles; and there is a resumé of Ballynakill life at the turn of the century: language, craftsmen, shops and shopping, agriculture and fishing, social life, wakes, games and sports all being covered.

The twentieth century is represented by appendices on local wild life and the meanings of the townlands' names in the parish.

Even if such a book does not exist for a parish in which one is interested, a study of *Portrait of a Parish* or a similar work by dedicated, if amateur, local and family historians, should give a good idea of what would have been happening in similar parishes all over Ireland at any given time in their history. Alternatively, instead of restricting one's attentions to one's own family, or giving up completely when the trail of a specific individual runs cold, the enterprising researcher could do worse than write his own 'portrait of a parish'.

Note-taking

Most of us probably think we have had plenty of experience in taking notes, from primary school days onwards. Many family historians, unfortunately, have found out to their cost that this is in fact something of an acquired art. The Society of Genealogists in London obviously agree, for their Leaflet No. 4 entitled 'Note-taking', goes into the subject in detail.

The gist of their advice is to take every chance of jotting down every reference you can possibly lay hands on; think ahead about what might be of use in the future, because, for reasons unknown, you may never have the chance again.

Proven facts should be kept separate from your own surmises and calculations, and the sources of these facts noted with them.

Exactly what is written should be copied down, leaving nothing out. Do not ever 'correct' anything, as a seeming mistake could offer a vital clue in differentiating between similar people. The writer is likely to have known the ancestor and his family personally, and there may be a clue in there somewhere for you.

Try not to abbreviate, or if you find this necessary for reasons of time or space, evolve a foolproof system whereby you will be certain of exactly what you read, a year, or a decade, afterwards. If not, you are almost certain to have trouble with similar names, such as Eliza and Elizabeth, Joseph, Joshua, and Josiah, for example.

Take care with Latin names, and be aware of the pitfalls of anglicization. Jacobus can indeed be Jacob, but it is more likely to be James; Johanna can be Joan, or Jane, and so on.

If you come across a word which you just cannot decipher, try to copy it out as exactly as possible even if it looks like Arabic at the time. Light may dawn at a later point, or someone else may be able to help.

Before you return the document, check that your note-taking contains no ambiguities which could trap you later. If you cannot make complete sense of it now, you certainly will not be able to in a few months' time. By the end of this preparation for the long trail into the past, some essential details will be needed which, it is hoped, will lead to the discovery of several generations of ancestors in their home parish in Ireland. The most crucial of these will, if dealing with the almost compulsory emigrant ancestor, be the following:

Surname.
Christian names; use care as regards their use, and the use of
    nicknames.
Occupations.
Religion; once again, things may not be as they seem,
    particularly where pressure has been brought to 'belong'
    to the Church of Ireland.
Home town; the County in Ireland will not be sufficient. A
    clue may sometimes be found in the new home town which
    may have been named after the Irish original. Check with
    a good gazetteer.
Dates of events searched for; these need to be as exact as
    possible.

The Public Record Office of Ireland (now called the National Archives) offers some advice in this respect.

The name of the family may not be quite so obvious as first appears. Some Celtic Irish surnames were either anglicized or actually translated into English: for instance, 'Goff' became Smith, quite unrecognizable to anyone not an expert in the field. It might be worth investigating whether several forms of the surname in question were in use at one time. Edward MacLysaght's *Irish Families* gives some startling examples of the different forms which may be found of something which would once have been the same surname, or, conversely, of one surname which now stands for several different ones.

If research is being done in the female line, keep in mind the fact that girls, even today, are sometimes referred to by their maiden names, even after decades of married life, by people who knew them as youngsters. Thus Kate O'Sullivan may still be known as such, although she was transformed into Mrs Kathleen Donovan many years ago. In the Celtic world more interest was taken in the blood line than is general in Anglo-Saxon regions; this explains why some Scottish ladies continue to be addressed by their maiden names after marriage, and probably why many Americans use the surnames of both the father and the husband. Strangely enough, though, in both Britain and Germany it is not compulsory for the bride to take the groom's surname on marriage, although it is most unusual for her not to do so.

Ask around among older members of the family, and friends, for ideas about any other surnames which they associate with that of your family. They may be the same name in disguise, be ones that have intermarried with your own at some point, or at least have come from the same town or village.

Unless you are researching a very unusual name, or one which is distinguished and therefore well-documented, the county of origin is unlikely to be of much assistance, in view of the fact that, even today in Ireland, surnames tend to be more concentrated in certain parts of the country, as has already been discussed.

The date will probably have to remain approximate, having been arrived at by intelligent deduction or guesswork, unless the ancestor can be pinpointed at some exact time. If he was an emigrant, obviously this can provide most useful pointers, such as when he left Ireland, or set foot in his new country. The best you may be able to manage is guesswork based on a calculation of when he and his family disappear from Irish records, or start to appear in those of the country of adoption.

If unsuccessful in an attempt to establish the exact place of origin, try:

The Computer File Index of the Mormon Church (CFI) on
  microfiche
Tithe Applotment Books
Primary (or Griffith's) Valuation Books
Calendars of Wills and Administrations
Index to pre-1858 Wills
Index to Marriage Licence Bonds pre-1864
Various Card Indexes

– all of which are available in the Public Record Office of Ireland, and will be described in more detail later in this book.

It is equally important to note when nothing has been found. In that case the source studied plus the date it was consulted should be recorded, both to avoid going over the same ground twice, and to take advantage of future developments (like finding an easy-to-read transcription) which could make all the difference.

Note what the document was checked for, and how thoroughly you were able to go through it. If you did not do so word by word, there is a good chance that something has been missed, or that you were not looking for clues which might be important as your research progresses.

Mention in your notes if the source is faulty in any way, if there are gaps in the text, or damage, or if part of it has been destroyed. Similarly, note whether you were using the original or a copy.

Against each entry which you find of relevance to your family, record the source, and in what form it was studied: original, transcript, microfilm or fiche extract. Something more modern or more accurate may become available later, and throw light on your doubts and problems.

Keep all your findings in loose-leaf files rather than in note-books or exercise books. Files may be expanded and re-arranged at will as the research progresses, and other leads, such as inter-married families, may be interposed. When transferring details onto your files, use the same format, kept in the same order.

At all times keep an open mind about alternative spellings, Christian names, and nicknames, and do not discard anything out of hand because it does not agree immediately with something which you believe to be absolutely certain. Even official sources can and do contain mistakes, often serious ones, Civil Registration certificate copies and Census Returns being notorious offenders in this respect.

Lastly, and most importantly, enjoy what you are doing, and take a pride in your achievements, however slow your progress!

THE ANCESTOR ABROAD:
THE BRITISH MAINLAND

It is not within the scope of this book to cover every aspect of family history in England, Scotland and Wales. The Welsh system, for example, is so similar to the English, that it needs no separate explanation, while that in Scotland is so different as to warrant a book to itself. This is mainly due to the differing legal systems of Scotland, on the one hand, and England and Wales on the other.

Those who are interested in examining the research sources in mainland Britain in detail should consult a specialist publication, of which their are many good examples on the market. Family historians with a particular interest in Scottish genealogy should read G. K. S. Hamilton-Edwards's *In Search of Scottish Ancestry*, Chichester, Phillimore 1974, or the more recent *Scottish Family History*, by David Moody, published by Batsford in 1988.

This chapter will not include details of the various less important sources available to the British family historian: Irish ancestors may well be found therein, but in small numbers. Those with access to local newspapers, estate, school, club, society or hospital papers and records; Quarter Session records; apprenticeship indentures; and parish records of any description in local repositories where their Irish ancestor is known to have lived or stayed in mainland Britain, should, of course, make the best of every opportunity which presents itself.

On the other hand, the major sources – parish registers, the Census, Civil Registration and wills – have been mentioned here. This is because the vast majority of Irish immigrants to the United Kingdom will feature in at least one of them, if not all four. In addition, ancestors from both the top and the bottom of the social scale are likely to appear in them, either as servants, seasonal workers, paupers, wrong-doers or emigrants, or at the other extreme, as wealthy landowners, with property in both countries.

In addition, the English and Welsh sources were the forerunners of those in the other English-speaking countries, and in most cases are more detailed and in a better state of preservation; this is not, unfortunately, true of the Civil Registration system which in the New World is generally superior to ours, but it is certainly so of the Census and, of course, of parish registers and records which normally go back to at least Stuart times. It is for this reason, as well as the fact that Irishmen have been coming to England for centuries, that they have been covered in greater detail than those of the other countries to which the Irish emigrated in any numbers.

Emigration to mainland Britain

Because migration and emigration to Britain have been so general and so widespread, the Irish appear in many records and documents housed on the mainland, and the Irish in Britain are considered here at greater length than their relations elsewhere in the English-speaking world.

With the Act of Union of 1800 and the subsequent loss of the Irish Parliament, what little industry did exist in Ireland, which was mainly in the Belfast area, suffered from overwhelming competition from the rapidly-developing English economy. This led to a rise in the immigration rate to England's larger industrial towns, already overcrowded by more workers than they could safely accommodate.

In addition to the demand for labour in the 'Workshop of the World', as England was able to style itself in the nineteenth century, generations of Irish workers had already been coming to the mainland in search of casual and seasonal work, at the same time keeping close links with other Irish people who had already left for good.

Flora Thompson, the author of *Lark Rise to Candleford*, a description of village life in north Oxfordshire and Buckinghamshire towards the end of the Victorian era, had been used to seeing Irish harvesters during her childhood. They were paid on piecework, and would labour until dusk. A threat to local children who refused to behave took the form of 'I'll give you to them old Irishers!' in much the same way that South Coast children would be threatened with 'Boney', but Flora, who came to know them as individuals during the course of her work in the Post Office, saw them in quite a different light.

They would send part of their wages home in postal orders and stopped for a chat with the Post Office assistant, who found them to be '... men who did no-one harm beyond irritating them by talking too much and working harder and by doing so earning more money than they did.' The Irishmen '... came for a season, as the swallows came, then disappeared across the sea to a country called "Ireland" where people wanted Home Rule and said "Begorra", and made things called "bulls", and lived exclusively upon potatoes.' None of the older ones could write – neither could my own great-grandmother, who, born in Bermondsey in 1850, nevertheless managed to own shares and property – the younger ones having to do it for them. Sometimes Flora herself was called upon to write messages from dictation to those back home in Ireland. When doing so, she noticed that 'words came freely to the Irishman, and there were rich, warm phrases in his letters that sounded like poetry. What Englishman of his class would think of wishing his wife could live like a queen?'

The Irishmen, too, had better manners than their English counterparts: 'said "plaze" more frequently, doffed their caps at the door', and were 'almost effusive' in their thanks.

Apart from these harvesters and their colleagues, the construction industry in Britain owes a great debt to those Irishmen who left their homes and families to work on such undertakings as the London Underground, the motorway system, and countless building sites throughout the country; the latest generation is, even at this moment, working away on the Channel Tunnel.

Neither must it be forgotten that the Irish were British until as recently as 1921, even though they lived across the sea on 'John Bull's Other Island', as Shaw put it. In addition to this centuries-old link, both countries are still locked together as fellow members of the EEC, but, even before their joint entry in 1973, bringing with it a mutual obligation to do so, Irish workers needed no work permit in the United Kingdom and were given the vote on arrival in the country.

Even if they had no intention of leaving Ireland permanently, hundreds of Irish people, or those of Irish parentage, found their way into British family history records by virtue of having been born, baptized, married, died, or got themselves into the record-book in some way or another while over here.

By the early 1960s, over one million persons of Irish birth were living in England, where they fitted in with the native population almost unnoticed. However, this flood of immigrants began to be reduced to a trickle by the end of that decade.

In his book *The Irish*, Brian Cleeve states that the Irish are still very interested in the British Royal Family, even though they have been deprived of them for nearly seventy years. Do they, perhaps, like the citizens of the United States, have a certain sense of something being missing, some personality with which to identify?

Donall Mac Amhlaigh, who came to live in England in 1951, wrote of his memories of St Patrick's Day in Ireland, in the St Patrick's Day edition of *Ireland's Own* magazine, in the column entitled 'The Irish Abroad'. One day he went to a 'Paddy's Day' dance in Northampton and, in a local pub, was asked if he were Polish! The explanation was as follows: 'Well, he speaks like a Pole – I can't understand a word 'e says.' Even today, says the writer, he has to moderate his speech as he 'can't quite manage an English accent', and 'I find it necessary sometimes to tone down my own accent if I wish to be understood.' So much for Anglo-Irish understanding. Incidentally, the place in which to spend 17 March during the 1950s was London, where there were large numbers of Irish youngsters.

In the same edition of *Ireland's Own* there is a letter saying that, in California, its writer learned from Mr Mac Amhlaigh's articles 'that England is a good country to live in', an amusing compliment to the traditional enemy, even if paid behind their back. For their own part, the English are learning to accept this Celtic cuckoo in their midst, and at least to acknowledge its particular brand of culture. In the current edition of a brochure published to advertise the attractions of London's newly-fashionable Dockland, mention is made of St Patrick's Church, Green Bank, Wapping, E1. This Roman Catholic building, it says, was built in 1879 from penny-a-week contributions made by the congregation, mainly Irish immigrants, as its name suggests.

Similarly, Oxford, not exceptionally well-known for its Irish population, has had a series of Irish Festivals, which seem all set to become an annual event. Even the four-star Randolph Hotel, which normally limits its ethnic awareness to the tastes of rich Americans, has offered Irish cuisine in its Coffee Shop for the week of the Festival. Items included Potato and Onion Soup, Irish Stew, and Guinness Cake. Also available were smoked Irish salmon, iced soufflé flavoured with Bailey's, a folk group and Irish cocktails. The Festival itself involved the local Member of Parliament (an Englishman) the Irish Embassy, Aer Lingus and many local public houses, while the sizeable programme carried advertisements from such bodies as the Oxford Football and

Hurling Club, Eire Óg. Raffle prizes were tickets for events such as céilídhs and even trips back to Ireland. What was so heartening about this particular Festival was the fact that the Irish organizers were at pains to include the local English community in its celebrations and to explain anything which they thought might be a mystery to the Anglo-Saxon mind.

The importance of Liverpool in the history of emigration

Between 1830 and 1930 about 40 million people left Europe for what they hoped would be a better life in North America and Australasia. Liverpool was their principal port of departure due, initially, to its centuries-old trade links with North America.

The early days of Liverpool's history as a port saw departures chiefly for Ireland, North America and the West Indies. Although only in small numbers initially, it has been used for emigration and immigration since the late-seventeenth century.

After 1800 emigration increased, and by 1830 some 15,000 people were leaving Liverpool each year. Perhaps even more significantly for those interested in Irish ancestors, thousands of Irish people spent all their savings and capital on actually reaching Liverpool and could afford to go no further. In addition, many more must have decided to stay on there with family and friends, instead of taking the risky step of emigrating overseas to more exotic places. In Liverpool then, they could be abroad, but among their own people still.

In the course of the nineteenth century, ships would arrive from abroad laden with cargoes such as cotton and timber and return with English goods and passengers. After 1830, communications to Liverpool became good enough for people from all over Britain to assemble there before departing; and not only from Britain, but also from the Baltic countries, via Hull.

The numbers of emigrants increased steadily over the decades to reach a peak in the 1880s. The main shipping companies carrying passengers from the port were Cunard, White Star, National, Inman, Guion, Dominion, Anchor and Allan. A breakdown of those passengers leaving in 1889, for example, shows that 196,000 went to the United States, 36,000 to Canada and 18,000 to Australia. Of all those who emigrated via Liverpool overall, that is, not just from the United Kingdom, 7 million went to the States,

59

1½ million to Canada, ¾ million to Australia and lesser numbers to New Zealand, South Africa and South America.

After 1890, however, Liverpool's supremacy declined as the flood of emigrants from Northwestern Europe slowed down and those from the Mediterranean countries and Eastern Europe began to take their place. Increasing competition was experienced from ports such as Southampton, Hamburg and Bremen, who were better situated to deal with the later departures.

The outbreak of the Great War in 1914 stopped all emigration and after it was over the numbers of emigrants were curbed by new registration laws passed in North America. By 1930, only a few thousand were leaving each year from Liverpool, although those numbers were increased for a time by GI brides after the Second World War.

Liverpool remains to this day a centre of Irishness. From 1885 until 1929 it actually returned an Irish Nationalist MP for one of its constituencies and it had four Protestant Party councillors in the Town Hall in 1971. After Partition, the Irish Catholic vote in Liverpool went Labour, possibly because Catholics were usually refused admittance to Conservative clubs. Ironically, the word 'Tory' is Irish in origin (seventeenth-century from 'tóraidhe', meaning 'outlaw') and was first applied to Irish Catholics, especially outlaws, who preyed upon English settlers.

Today, when little more than the Irish ferries use the once-teeming docks, there is still a link which is immediately apparent in Liverpool surnames, and in the accent, social and religious life and the sense of humour of the city which produced Lennon and McCartney, both good Irish names.

The 'Emigrants to a New World' exhibition in Merseyside Maritime Museum

This permanent exhibition contains specific reference to Irish emigrants, with a 1/12 scale model of an Irish village, its construction based on evidence from contemporary sources. Set in the 1840s, it shows villagers dismayed by their diseased potato patch. Others are getting ready to leave for the United States. Liverpool street scenes, models of actual ships, recorded extracts from a passenger's diary kept during his voyage to Australia in the 1850s, and many other items, combine with video presentations which use original archive film to make everything come alive.

The most memorable feature, however, is the reconstruction of Victorian dockland areas, with the processes involved in emigrating.

The visitor makes his way along a dimly-lit brick alley-way, to the sounds and smells of spit-and-sawdust taverns, in order to reach the doorway of an emigrant lodging-house ('Good beds 4d per day'). Here, a prospective guest fends off a snarling dog, with the help of his walking-stick.

The next scene is a transit shed, filled with luggage for the crossing, and then a reconstruction of a section of the steerage accommodation of a sailing ship, in this case the *Shackamaxon*. This was an American packet of the early 1850s, which did first the trans-Atlantic, then the Australian run.

In the darkness, relieved only by lanterns which the more well-prepared emigrants have remembered to bring along with them, it is hard to distinguish between 'passengers', attendants and fellow-visitors. The claustrophobic effect is heightened by accompanying sounds of groaning timbers, the crash of waves and even the vomiting of sea-sick emigrants.

In complete contrast is the computerized Emigration Bureau, which lists those sources of importance to people in search of emigrant ancestors, taking the process step by step. The Merseyside Maritime Museum produces three information packs, *Tracing Your Emigrant Ancestors in Australia and New Zealand, . . . in the United States and Canada*, and *. . . in the United Kingdom and Eire*, which contain the computer programme on printed cards and are on sale in the exceptionally well-stocked museum shop.

Also of interest is the souvenir guide from the exhibition, written by Michael Hall (1986). Produced by National Museums and Galleries on Merseyside, it is the source of most of the above information.

Documents in the Public Record Office which relate to emigrants

The most helpful of the PRO's leaflets, when considering emigrant ancestors, is Number 7. For those interested in Irish ancestry, leaflets Number 6 on Immigrants and Number 3 on Records of the Royal Irish Constabulary, should also be noted. Documents concerning emigrants are, for the main part, housed at the Kew branch of the PRO.

Unfortunately for the family historian, there is no single index of names of emigrants; nor, as a rule, are the British divided up into separate nationalities unless the documents in question refer to a particular area.

Apart from the more obvious class of emigrants, those who intended leaving Britain for good, there were many others whose occupations or circumstances involved stays overseas, either temporary or prolonged. The PRO's sources, therefore, tend to deal with wrong-doers, services personnel, Crown and Government officials and businessmen, rather than ordinary working people. However, all the documents of those Government departments which were involved with pre-Partition Ireland, such as the State Papers of Ireland and, indeed, the Irish Army records, are held by the PRO. On the creation of the Irish Free State in 1922, many official records were brought over to London and so escaped destruction.

The chief sources of interest are the various types of Colonial Office records (Class No. CO at Kew). Emigration Lists for the century 1600 to 1700 have largely been transcribed and are already in print. Lesser numbers of Home Office (HO) and Board of Trade (BT) as well as Treasury papers (T) which are all housed at Kew, mention emigrants.

Much of the material listed above has been published and is available in the PRO's Search Department; it has also been partially listed, in various degrees of completeness, by societies and individual researchers. The *Guide to Contents of the Public Record Office*, in 3 volumes published by HMSO, gives an outline of the different classes of record, but those relating to individuals are listed in leaflet No. 7, already mentioned above.

Examples of useful records are those belonging to the Home Office (HO 11) 1787–1871 which run to 21 volumes of Convict Transportation Registers; and HO 10, dealing with convicts sent to New South Wales and Tasmania, in 64 volumes, which constitute a form of census between the years 1788 and 1859 and which also list 'free' emigrants and persons actually born in Australia.

From Board of Trade records come Passenger Lists Outwards (BT 27) which are listings of those leaving the United Kingdom by sea as detailed by the ships' masters and sent in to the Minister of Trade. None of these, though, is earlier than 1890, but all exist for subsequent years. These listings are arranged by year, under the port of departure, and usually give age, occupation and last place of residence; none of them is indexed.

It should be emphasized, however, that the Public Record Office's leaflets and listings are several years out of date and, as with any large repository and its publications, should serve only to give an indication of the type of record available. As such places are constantly acquiring and updating their material, lack of mention does not necessarily mean that a particular document is not held.

Irish material in major British libraries

The largest and most important library in Britain is the British Library, formerly known as the Library of the British Museum. At present it occupies a site in Bloomsbury, but plans are afoot to transfer it to the King's Cross area in the early 1990s.

The British Library is one of six copyright libraries in the British Isles (the others are the Bodleian Library, Oxford; Cambridge University Library; the National Libraries of Scotland and Wales, in Edinburgh and Aberystwyth, respectively; and Trinity College Library, in Dublin). All these libraries are entitled to a free copy of any book published in Britain, although they do not automatically take up this privilege, for reasons of space. Until 1922, therefore, the copyright libraries were entitled to Irish books and have built up a large stock of Irish material over the years.

The department of the British Library which would be of most service to the Irish family historian is the Official Publications and Social Sciences Service (the OP and SS) formerly known as the O.P.L. or Official Publications Library.

Principal holdings of direct relevance include:

Irish Electoral Registers
Of some 7,500 pre-1922 registers, only 8 are held; these date from 1885/6 and come from the Borough of Newry (Co. Down), Co. Fermanagh South Division, and Co. Tyrone North, Mid, East and South Divisions; for 1887 there is Westmeath North and South Divisions.

Post-Partition holdings are 5 registers for Dublin for the 1938 Dáil elections.

For Northern Ireland, post-Partition, there are no registers, virtually, before 1947 except for one from 1937 and, indeed, none was compiled between 1940 and 1944.

Griffith's or Primary Valuation
The British Library owns micro-film and micro-form copies of the Valuation and also Parish Indexes, the 1861 Census Report which was published in 1863, and an index of places mentioned. Micro-film copies of the Valuation are held elsewhere in Britain as well.

House of Commons Sessional Papers
Although the House of Lords Library acts as the archive for both Houses of Parliament, parliamentary publications and indexes are not rare. The British Library has various editions: microcard, microfiche, and a selective reprint of material relating to Ireland by the Irish Universities Press, much of which is also available in larger libraries, particularly university ones, thoughout Britain. Complete sets of Papers are accessible to the general public, without the necessity of obtaining a reader's ticket, at both the Westminster Central Reference Library and the Guildhall Library of the City of London.

As for the British Library itself, admission to the sections most relevant to the study of Irish family history, namely the OP and SS, the Map Room and the Department of Printed Books, is by pass and personal application. This normally only takes a few minutes and the ticket is normally issued for a fortnight in the first instance.

For fuller details of Irish material held by the British Library, see two articles in *Family Tree Magazine*, the first by Bill Davis in Vol. 4, No. 9, July 1988, the second by R. H. A. Cheffins of the OP and SS, in Vol. 5, No. 3, January 1989.

Miscellaneous indexes

Besides official repositories, private individuals and societies have also compiled indexes and listings, some of one particular family, others for certain areas, or from publications. Announcements and offers of help are frequently advertised in family history journals and magazines such as *Family Tree Magazine*.

A particularly useful set of indexes would seem to be that compiled by Mr Peter Manning of 18 Stratford Avenue, Rainham,

Kent, which contains over 100,000 names. These have been taken from:

34 copies of the journal *Irish Ancestor* 1969–1986
54 copies of the *Irish Genealogist* 1937–1986
The Irish Patent Rolls of James I, 1603–1625
The 1749 Religious Census for the Diocese of Elphin
Freeholders of Co. Roscommon 1768–1799
1,000 Soldiers stationed at Chatham in 1851
Persons of Irish birth from the Censuses of Chatham 1841 to 1881 inclusive.

Enquirers should send four first-class stamps or the equivalent, plus return envelope.

Civil Registration

In *England and Wales* Civil Registration began in 1837 for Births, Marriages and Deaths. Information and copies of certificates may be obtained from the Register Office where the event was registered originally, or from St Catherine's House, 10 Kingsway, London WC1B 6JB. From 25 July 1988, postal applications (only) are dealt with from Smedley Hydro, Southport, Merseyside, where applicants will be referred in future by St Catherine's House.

The following details should be included on English and Welsh certificates:

Birth Certificates
Surname and Christian Name(s) if already chosen; Names and Address of the Parents; the Father's Occupation; Mother's Maiden Name; the Name of the Informant, who is normally one of the parents.

Marriage Certificates
Date and Place of the Ceremony; Names of the Parties and their Ages (at least 'Full' or 'Minor'); Occupations; Marital Status; Addresses; Names of the Fathers with any mention if one is deceased; Signatures or Marks of the Couple and of the Witnesses and person officiating.

Death Certificates

Name and Address of the Deceased; Age; Cause of Death; Name of the Informant and their relationship to the Deceased.

In *Scotland* Civil Registration began in 1855 and the central repository is New Register House, Edinburgh EH1 3YT.

Scottish certificates are fuller than English or Welsh ones, particularly for the year 1855. Unfortunately, this initial system was found much too cumbersome to continue, and so later certificates are less full. Information found on Scottish certificates includes:

Birth Certificates

1855 only: as English ones, plus Parents' Ages and Birthplaces; Number of Offspring, both living and dead; Date and Place of the Parents' Marriage. Post-1855: as English certificates, but plus the Date and Place of the Parents' Marriage. For the years 1856 to 1861, however, the marriage details are not given.

Marriage Certificates

1855 only: as English ones, plus Places of Current Residence; any Former Marriages; Number of Children, alive or dead.

Post-1855: as English certificates, but with Names and Maiden Names of the Couple's Mothers.

Death Certificates

1855 only: Place of Birth; Details of any Marriages; Place of Burial; Names of all Offspring, alive or dead; plus usual details on English certificates.

Post-1855: as England and Wales, but with the addition of names of both Parents of the Deceased; and the Mother's Maiden Name.

As can be imagined, the details shown on the Civil Registration certificate are likely to contain errors and suppositions, particularly in regard to details of a deceased person's parentage and children. Mistakes also occur fairly frequently in copies of original entries, and so, if you are certain that the information which you already have is correct, do not amend it to conform with this, or any other type of official document. Details of immigrants are especially likely to be suspect due to cultural differences and the possible lack of close family or friends to provide accurate information.

Births, Marriages and Deaths at Sea

The travelling Irish are likely to have been recorded in one or more of the above categories. Original registers are kept at the PRO's Kew premises, while indexes are to be found at St Catherine's House, London.

Holdings are as follows:

General Births, Marriages and Deaths at Sea	1854 to 1883
Births and Deaths	1884 to 1887
Deaths	1888 onwards

Those of British Nationals only (including Irish)

Births	1874
Deaths	1874

The Census

English and Welsh Census Returns on microfilm are on view at the Public Record Office's Land Registry Building, Portugal Street WC2. The Search Room is open between 9.30 a.m. and 5.30 p.m. and either a PRO reader's ticket or a day pass, obtainable at the door, is necessary for entry.

The PRO Guide No. 18 *Searching the Census* is given to the researcher on arrival, but it is wise to obtain and study a copy in advance, if this is at all possible. One can waste much valuable time feeling one's way, or making the bad mistake of looking up details of the microfilm which one needs, before booking a reader, for example, as it is not posible to order a film without giving a reader number.

English and Welsh censuses were taken every ten years, with the exception of 1941, owing to the War. Those which are of interest to the family historian are those compiled from 1841 onwards as, although census returns do exist from before that date, they give no details of individuals.

The 1841 returns give less information and have suffered more wear and tear in many cases than their successors. For instance, the exact age and place of birth are not generally given; the ages are approximate, rounded down to the nearest five years; and the county, or even country, of birth is given instead of the town or village. Those not born in England or Wales are in Ireland's case marked by the initial of the country, a capital 'I'. These appear in the far right-hand columns.

In the returns from 1851 onwards, the exact age and place of birth should be shown, although of course the enumerator was at the mercy of his informants and had no means, or inclination, to verify the information given.

Many microfilm copies of the returns exist, countrywide, in libraries and in the possession of local family history societies. J. S. W. Gibson's *Census Returns 1841–51–61–71–1881 on Microfilm: A Directory of Local Holdings*, published by the Federation of Family History Societies and updated regularly, is a great asset in ascertaining the whereabouts of microfilm copies throughout the country.

Scottish censuses may be consulted at Edinburgh's New Register House. Although there are certain advantages in coming to Portugal Street and having a nationwide range of returns at one's disposal, so that one may work one's way from county to county, it is more comfortable and convenient to conduct one's search at a local level.

The Portugal Street Search Room is usually very crowded, with time wasted queuing for a reader, and waiting for the film to arrive. No advance bookings are accepted and should a coach party of enthusiasts beat you to it, bent on a whole day's research, a trip to London could be in vain.

Some family or local history societies have already transcribed and indexed parishes, if not entire villages, and so it is better to enquire of one of these if the area in which you are interested has already been dealt with. Although nothing can replace the sense of achievement experienced when the quarry is run to ground, it will save time and money to consult an index, or send a stamped addressed envelope with a request for someone else to do so. Another advantage of consulting any sort of historical source in its own area, is that local people will be at hand to answer queries about distances and relationships between communities and there will be at least a detailed map for you to use.

When using the Census, it is necessary to have as exact an address as possible; a county would take months of back-breaking labour to work through, while a city is possible to deal with but very difficult. Small villages on the other hand may not have complete addresses, only streets, roads, or even numbers. If you can, have a look at a directory such as Kelly's, to give an idea of the area at a certain point in time.

Bear in mind that, like anything else compiled by human beings, there is likely to be a fair amount of error in the information contained on returns. Many people would genuinely not have known the answers to what they were being asked; others would not have understood the questions in the first place; while others perhaps feared that they would be sent back whence they came, or wished to cover up a skeleton in the family cupboard.

Mistakes and misunderstandings were bound to arise, particularly when the enumerator and his informant spoke with markedly different accents or when the former was faced with names and places which he had never heard of before. This would have been especially true in the case of recent Irish immigrants, many of whom had had very little experience of form-filling at either first or second hand. Thus, different years' returns may well contain quite widely differing information.

On mainland Census returns entries for Irish ancestors could well list them as lodgers, living in someone else's house in transit for better things in the New World, or with relatives or friends. These are more likely to be found in ports and coastal towns to the west and south of England, such as Liverpool or Southampton, or on Clydeside in Scotland. Other Irish people, perhaps longer established in the country, may be listed as servants, nurses or labourers, also living in English households.

Further up the social scale, one sometimes finds Irish professional men raising their families in England, like the Dublin-born brood of the Reverend and Mrs Carey, who ministered to both the spiritual and bodily needs of a tiny, rural congregation at Spelsbury, Oxfordshire. The reverend gentleman bore the same surname as my mother's family and was to officiate, by strange coincidence, at the wedding of the ancestors of my Canadian cousins.

Although finding an ancestor on a Census return provides several invaluable details about his or her life, unfortunately he or she may have only been staying at that address for a night or two in March or April when the Census was taken and may therefore have had little or nothing to do with the community in which the name appears. On the other hand, though, you may be on to a clue which will take you straight back to Ireland in one bound.

English and Welsh Parish Registers

English and Welsh registers were inaugurated in accordance with an injunction made by Thomas Cromwell in 1538. This Thomas was a minister of Henry VIII and, although of the same family, is not to be confused with the 'Bloody Owd' Cromwell who was destined to wreak so much havoc in Ireland. Of these early registers, very few survivors remain, for the majority were in loose-leaf form.

In 1598 parchment books were ordered to be purchased by each parish, and earlier entries to be copied into them. Unfortunately, the order was only made for this to be done from Elizabeth I's accession in 1558, not back to 1538, and many of the original sheets were destroyed when the parchment books were bought, without the entire collection of entries being copied.

Contents and upkeep of registers vary every few years, for they are at the mercy of the compiler who might or might not be competent or conscientious. The majority are in fairly good condition, and have not suffered too much from wear, tear and decay, considering their age and the less-than-ideal conditions in which they have been stored.

During the years 1640 to 1660, that is from the first rumblings of the Civil Wars until the Restoration, virtually all registers are faulty, and have breaks during the Commonwealth period from 1649 to 1660. At this time an official known as the Lay Register was employed and civil marriages were in force. For this reason, one is fortunate if one is able to keep track of one's family during those troubled times.

The mid-seventeenth-century registers not infrequently show entries for the baptism of travellers' children, or for those of children of soldiers, some of which are likely to be Irish, although the names themselves are frequently unknown. It is unusual, though, to find Irish 'respectable' families settled in England or Wales until a much later date, unless they are members of the professional or aristocratic classes with land or business in both countries.

From the end of the seventeenth century, and through the following one, the Penal Laws were in effect, and many Catholics were forced to attend Anglican services in order to protect themselves and their families. It should not be assumed, therefore, that all entries in parish registers automatically refer to Anglican parishioners.

In the September of 1752 Britain, including Ireland, changed from the Julian to the Gregorian Calendar and the 3rd of September became the 14th, in order to bring the country into line with the rest of Europe in its dating system. Furthermore, the year was to begin on 1st January instead of 25th March, Lady Day. This is the reason why parish registers, as well as many other sources and copies, show a 'double' year if the date fell between 1st January and Lady Day, e.g. 19th February 1603/4.

Hardwicke's Marriage Act, which came into force in 1755, aimed to prevent runaway and clandestine weddings, marriages only being legal after the calling of banns, or the obtaining of a licence. Although the Act principally affected those who had evil designs upon the wealth of a minor, or young couples marrying without the consent of parent or guardian, it is also important for those researchers with Roman Catholic or Presbyterian ancestry. According to the Act, all marriages, apart from those of Quakers and Jews, were to be valid only if performed by an Anglican clergyman. This meant that there was even less tolerance of Catholics and Non-Conformists in England than in Ireland. It is sensible, therefore, to look in Church of England registers, even if one is sure that one's ancestors were of a different persuasion, for there may well have been both an Anglican and a Catholic ceremony, the latter, of course, having taken place before the former.

After 1755, new register books were bought, in ready-made printed form, with four marriages to the page. Entries now included signatures, or marks, of both parties, plus those of the officiating clergyman and the witnesses.

It was not until George Rose's Act of 1813 that the keeping of three separate registers became compulsory. Until then events were likely to be a hotch-potch under the same year, only marriages being separated after 1755. After 1813 baptisms were to include the names, addresses and description or status of the parents, and burials the name, age, address and occupation of the deceased.

This is the state of affairs today, and how it would have been during the period when the vast majority of Irish emigrants arrived in mainland Britain, in the course of the nineteenth and twentieth centuries. The above brief history of English and Welsh registers gives some idea of how the average set of registers would have evolved in this country and shows how deficient Irish ones are likely to be in comparison. Indeed, English parish records are among the the best in the world and one is lucky if an Irish ancestor is mentioned in them, rather than having his activities remain unknown in his native land.

It is necessary to point out that, towards the end of the eighteenth century and throughout the nineteenth, the population of Britain was increasing at a very fast rate and new churches and chapels were being built to accommodate it. Some places had chapels-of-ease subservient to a mother church, but many more had newly-created parish churches. If the church to which one's ancestors went is a relatively modern one, it will be essential to establish the old parish of which the newer one was once part.

A very welcome step, and one which should be copied by other countries before priceless records are lost for ever, was the passing of the Parish Registers and Records Measure, which came into effect on 1st January 1979. This made it compulsory for historical documents such as registers to be housed in conditions where they would be safe from both vandalism and the ravages of time or weather; previously it was not uncommon for such records to have been damaged by damp, nibbled by mice, or ripped by ignorant persons. So high were the standards imposed that the great majority of parishes were compelled to deposit their treasures with the local County or Borough Record Office or Archives. Those that kept them in the parish were forced, not only to keep them safe, but to allow access to them for research purposes. According to the Measure, however, the incumbent is allowed to charge a fee for the privilege.

Because of the unique and fragile nature of these original registers, however, archivists very sensibly insist that, where at all practicable, researchers should use copies, rather than the originals. Family history societies have been very active in transcribing those for their own areas, and these should be available either on the open shelves of the local Record Office or central library, or in microfilm format. Much filming has already been done by the Mormon Church, while the Society of Genealogists' Library in London receives copies of virtually all transcriptions made.

Scottish parish records were started in 1558, but very few sixteenth-century examples survive. All existing registers are housed in the New Register House in Edinburgh, where they may be searched for a fee.

English Roman Catholic Registers and Other Sources

The earliest known Catholic register was begun in 1657 by the Franciscans in Birmingham; the earliest register extant, according to the *English Catholic Ancestor*, starts in 1684. The majority of early ones start in the eighteenth century. Most parishes had records which began in the form of a notebook for, at this time, being a proven Catholic was still a risky business on account of the Penal Laws which were in effect in England just as much as in Ireland.

The worst problems encountered when attempting to trace a Catholic ancestor in England, however, are in the years following the onset of the potato famines in Ireland in the 1840s, when many thousands of labourers left that country to look for work in mainland Britain.

London, not surprisingly, was the worst place in which to live, and in which to do research today, for the little courtyards and tenements, packed into every square yard and overcrowded with newcomers, often went unrecorded in official surveys and reports. Indeed, most of these slums have long since vanished without trace, while their secret, sordid little churches and chapels had no actual parish, and therefore few, if any, records. Surprisingly few modern Catholic parishes – only two – have evolved from those already in existence in the 1840s.

Help, however, is obtainable from a professional genealogist who has compiled abstracts from about 60 parishes situated north of the Thames and in Essex and he has also translated these records into English from their original Latin. Of the 30,000 or so marriages, 1837 to 1870, details include:

> Date; the majority of Fathers and at least the Christian name of the Mother; many give addresses and/or Irish county of origin.

These abstracts do not normally include the names of witnesses, though, unless they have the same surname as one of the parties involved.

A search fee is charged and a stamped addressed envelope, with enquiries may be sent to:

Father Godfrey Anstruther, O.P.,
c/o The Church Shop,
222 Leigh Road,
Leigh on Sea,
Essex.

Although English Roman Catholic registers normally remain in the care of the parish priest, some are kept by the Jesuits in their Archives at 114 Mount Street, London W1Y 6AH.

In addition to records actually compiled by members of the Catholic Church, there is a vast amount of material among the State papers of both England and Ireland which relates to Catholics, usually as law-breakers. Needless to say, these are not all necessarily Irishmen, for, although the Church of England became the official and Established Church under Henry VIII, not all Englishmen became converted and there remain to this day pockets of Catholicism, Lancashire being a leading example. The English themselves tend to think of Catholicism as an Irish, or Continental, denomination, probably because most of the Catholics they know are of Irish, Polish, Italian or other Mediterranean extraction, but one has only to think of the Duke of Norfolk and his family to realize that this is not always the case. Nevertheless, those who persisted in absenting themselves from the parish church and attending their own, be it Roman Catholic or Non-Conformist, chapel were breaking the law of the land and therefore punishable under it.

Since 1904 the Catholic Record Society has been engaged in transcribing and publishing all types of records and documents relative to the Catholic Church in this country. The Society issues a catalogue of their work, and also a journal named *Recusant History*. Details are obtainable from Miss R. Rendel, Catholic Record Society, c/o 43 Lansdowne Road, London W11 2LQ.

Besides the publishing of Catholic registers, the Society also deals with Recusant Rolls (lists of those fined for non-attendance at the parish church and the fines imposed, the originals of which are either in the County Record Offices or the Public Record Office) and Returns of Papists sent to the Bishop, many of which give occupation and residence.

Another journal which will be of interest to those with Catholic ancestors is the *English Catholic Ancestor*. Details of it, and the society which produces it, are available from the Hon. Secretary, Mrs B. H. Murray, 2 Winscombe Crescent, Ealing, London W5 1AZ.

The Scottish Record Office holds photocopies of the Catholic baptism, marriage and other registers from the eighteenth to the twentieth centuries.

Non-Conformist Sources

Although Protestant Non-Conformist sects were not looked on as a threat to national security as were the Roman Catholics, who were often seen as being in league with England's traditional enemies, France and Spain, any sort of non-Anglican was liable to a degree of persecution. The Baptists and the Quakers, in particular, were considered disturbers of the peace and suffered threats, fines and even imprisonment for their beliefs.

Religious censuses were carried out from time to time and the findings sent to the Bishop, so that we have some idea of the concentrations of Catholics and Non-Conformists in certain areas and their relationship to the rest of the community. A study of local history will show that, far from being the rather poverty-stricken sections of society which Catholics are often imagined to be, they were frequently of ancient and respected 'county' families; similarly Non-Conformists were steady, middle-class tradesmen, for the most part. On reflection this makes sense, for only those who were of sufficiently high social and economic standing in the parish would be in a position to flaunt their beliefs publicly and pay the fines which were thus incurred. Such ancestors, then, will probably be found elsewhere in local records.

The original registers kept by Non-Conformist congregations are usually with the Minister, or, in the case of the older registers, in the Public Record Office in Chancery Lane.

Welsh registers up until Civil Registration are in the PRO, later ones in the local County Record Office, or the National Library of Wales at Aberystwyth. Scottish ones are mainly in the Scottish Record Office, although some are with the Registrar General, in the New Register House.

Transcripts of many Non-Conformist registers have been completed by local and family history societies and may be found in Record Offices and central libraries.

Dates of commencement of registers vary from denomination

to denomination and from county to county. For the approximate dates and whereabouts, see *The Local Historian's Encyclopedia* by John Richardson, which lists English denominations by county. Presbyterian registers, for example, which are likely to be those most relevant to the Irish ancestor, cover the mid-seventeenth to the early twentieth centuries, and are housed in Chancery Lane.

Wills in England and Wales

This is a very complicated subject and one which calls for a specialist publication such as J. S. W. Gibson's *Wills and Where to Find Them* (1974).

The following, therefore, is only a brief outline which may serve to give some indication as to how to find out if a particular will exists and the details contained in it. Unless an Irish forebear was known to have owned land or property in mainland Britain, or definitely died and left descendants there, it is unlikely that the subject of British wills is going to crop up in one's family research.

Until 1857, when a Probate Act was passed, wills were proved in a variety of places, depending on where the testator's property lay. They were, however, always proved in an ecclesiastical court and not a civil one.

The most junior of these was the Archdeacon's court, which dealt with property held exclusively in the one Archdeaconry; if it extended to more than one, the will was proved by the Diocesan Court. If, though, more than one diocese was involved, it depended on whether or not these lay within the same Ecclesiastical Province, that is, either Canterbury or York. If the properties or land were indeed in the same Province, either the Prerogative Court of Canterbury (the P.C.C.) or that of York (the P.C.Y.) proved the will; if not the P.C.C. would do so as the senior Province.

To make things even more confusing, those people who had social aspirations would sometimes go to the P.C.C. even though there was no need to do so. The P.C.C. also dealt with wills made by persons dying abroad, or at sea.

P.C.C. wills from 1383 until 1857 are at the PRO, Chancery Lane, with indexes available in all leading libraries throughout the country. Those for the P.C.Y. from 1389 to 1857 are at the

Borthwick Institute of Historic Research, St Anthony Hall, York. For Welsh wills proved before 1857, apply to the National Library at Aberystwyth.

Wills from both countries, proved from 1858 onwards, are at the Principal Probate Registry at Somerset House, in London's Strand, where quarterly indexes of wills are on the open shelves. The wills themselves may be read and copies sent on after payment of a small charge.

Scottish Wills

Scottish wills are just as confusing as English ones, perhaps more so because of the different terminology involved. Wills are usually referred to as 'testaments', the difference between a will and a testament being that, strictly speaking, the former deals with real estate, the latter with personal belongings. Furthermore, testaments are 'confirmed', instead of being proved.

Commissary courts were set up in Scotland and these confirmed testaments from 1514 until 1823. The first of these courts was that of Edinburgh, which was actually established in 1514. The commissariats which the courts covered corresponded approximately with the medieval dioceses, while the jurisdiction of the Edinburgh court covered all of Scotland.

From 1854 onwards, the confirmation was done by Sheriffs' Courts and their records have been indexed.

The Scottish Record Society has published indexes of testaments up to 1800, the records of both the commissariat and the Sheriffs' Courts being held by the Scottish Record Office.

The Scottish system of land-ownership proves helpful to the historian, as land could be passed down only by inheritance, or by an act in law. Those documents which show entitlement to the possession of land are called 'sasines', and play an important role in family history research in Scotland.

In whatever country a will was proved, the fact should be borne in mind that the date of the making of a will and the date of probate may be quite different to the actual date of death. The testator may have made his will before going to sea, abroad, or to war, or during a serious illness from which he subsequently recovered. Similarly, it may have taken a matter of years for the will to be

77

proved if there had been some contention regarding its contents.

'All that glisters . . .' a cautionary tale

While I was at primary school, my mother happened to mention that her maiden name, Carey, was of Irish origin, or at least common in that country. As it was a convent school and there were plenty of Irish children, I was quite enthusiastic about the idea.

All that my mother knew about her family, never a particularly close one, was that she remembered her mother once telling her that a Carey, she presumed it was one of the family, had been involved 'in a war in Ireland'. As this would have been at some point prior to World War I, my grandmother had assumed this to be some sort of rebellion, but knew of no details whatsoever.

Some years later, while at grammar school, I was listening to a schools broadcast on the radio. It was of very little interest to me personally, as it concerned late-nineteenth-century Ireland, while I, at that time, rather fancied myself as a medievalist.

As I caught the name 'James Carey', however, I listened very carefully. The programme was about the Phoenix Park Murders which took place in May 1882. The Chief Secretary, Lord Frederick Cavendish and the Permanent Under-Secretary, Mr Burke, had been found dead in Dublin's Phoenix Park under very suspicious circumstances indeed.

This James Carey, who had been tried for the murders, turned Queen's Evidence and named his friends and associates to save his own skin. Five of them were publicly executed, but Carey himself, and his family, were acquitted on condition that, for his own safety, he emigrated to South Africa on board the *Melrose*. Before he was able to disembark, however, the informant was shot and killed by a fellow 'Invincible', one Patrick O'Donnell, on 29 July 1883, between Cape Town and Natal. O'Donnell was brought back to London and executed at Newgate Prison.

The intrigues leading up to the Phoenix Park Murders could well have been the 'war' to which my grandmother had referred, but where, exactly, did James Carey fit into our family? I just assumed that he was a distant relative, maybe a cousin who had stayed on in the 'Owd Sod', when my own branch came over to England.

Some twenty-five years later I took to researching my family history in earnest, although I was concentrating on my father's side of it. I did a little preliminary work on the Careys mainly because Jeff Carey, my first cousin, who at the time lived in Germany, wanted to know about them.

We still had no idea of where our family came from, still assuming tht it was Ireland and, out of curiosity, I wrote to the Genealogical Office in Dublin. In a few days I had a reply, informing me that:

> The gaelic O'Ciardha, from Ciar, meaning 'black hair', is the name of a family of the Southern Ui Neill who were, in gaelic times, Lords of Carbery in the present Co. Kildare. In addition, there are Careys of English origin in Ireland and these would be descendents of settler families mainly in the seventeenth century. Today the name is most numerous in Kildare, Meath and Westmeath.

Research in England revealed that our grandfather, Ernest George Carey, was born in Oxford in 1887, shortly after the time that James was busy being Invincible in Dublin and that Ernie's father, George William, was born in Worcester in 1860. Another generation back, and we found Edmund, Norfolk-born in 1826, and his father, Charles, who was born in my native Oxford in 1809. Before him came John, who was married there in 1808 and described in the parish register as 'of this parish'.

This took us back to the eighteenth century, but we were spoiled for choice as regards John's parentage and had to stop there, being unable to prove anything further.

Investigation on a more general level showed that there had been Careys all over Oxford, not merely surfacing in the eighteenth-century registers, but also in ones as far back as 1542, then medieval ones, including Richard, who was Mayor of Oxford in the fourteenth century.

By this time, it had become fairly obvious that our particular Careys, despite being extremely black-haired, were not likely to have been Irish at all, at any rate not for four centuries. Besides, Carey references had cropped up from all over the country, particularly in the Channel Isles, in Devon and in Cornwall.

Recently I received details of a convict who was transported to Australia as a punishment for breaking into houses in the dead of night and 'stealing thereout Linnen Aprons and Linnen Caps' with a 'linnen' handkerchief and other goods 'val. 10s. 3d.' The trial was at Taunton Castle in 1786, which makes the guilty party one of the first deportees Down Under.

The details were sent to me by Jeff Carey who, by this time, had himself emigrated to Sydney. What amused him about this report, which was a photocopy of a printed record giving full references from both Australia and the PRO was the fact that the convict's name was Ann Carey – the same as his sister! What it did show, however, was that there were plenty of Careys in Devon and Somerset, as well as in Ireland and Oxford, and it illustrates only too well the dangers of assuming that one may safely link together an 'Irish' name like Carey, and emigration to Australia.

THE ANCESTOR ABROAD:
THE NEW WORLD

As we have seen, British and Irish family history researchers are fortunate in that on the whole major sources such as the Census, or Civil Registration, start in the same year regardless of the part of the country in question. In North America and Australasia, however, it must be remembered that some states and provinces were settled long before others and that their records will naturally go much further back.

Although these earlier settlements have the obvious advantage of more extensive records, the newer ones usually remain closer to their roots in the British Isles and thus stay in touch with family and friends there. In this way they may benefit from more accurate information, in many cases obtained first or second hand, rather than having to rely upon somewhat dubious family traditions and surmises which are often based on wishful thinking.

Later emigrants lived in an era of better documentation and more general education and were better able to give an account of themselves and to keep abreast with what was going on in the Old World. Their children and grandchildren were able to absorb much of the culture and history of their ancestors naturally, and were not forced to study them as if they related to a foreign country.

Curiously, though, the reverse may be true of Irish ancestors, for those who left well before the panic and confusion of the famine years in the mid-nineteenth century were recorded as individuals rather than a mass of refugee humanity, herding as best it could into any vessel on board which a passage was available.

In the new country, registration could be undertaken in a more leisurely, and therefore more thorough, way than in Europe where the system had to be started from scratch, as elsewhere, but with a much larger population to contend with. Civil records in the New World, then, are generally fuller and better kept than in the Old.

The following chapter is, by necessity, only an outline of what is available in North America and the New World, with guidance about sources which differ from those of the British Isles. Sources not so described will be very similar to British and Irish ones, as in the case of parish registers, for example.

Sources for family history research

1. The United States of America

Because of the many textbooks available on American family history, it would be pointless to repeat in this book information which is widely published in the States. Instead an outline is given of those sources of immediate benefit to the researcher, namely: Passenger Arrival Records; Naturalization Records; Census Records; and the holdings of the Church of Jesus Christ of Latter-day Saints, or Mormons.

Probably the most important records one can use in researching the origins of immigrant ancestors to the United States are the passenger arrival records in the National Archives in Washington DC. Identifying, at a minimum, the country of origin of virtually every immigrant arriving in the States from 1820 onwards, they provide documentation on millions of individuals. As far as Irish arrivals are concerned they are a practically unique source of immigration data, for almost no official records of emigration from Ireland were ever kept.

An exciting new book on American passenger arrival records, by Michael Tepper, *American Passenger Arrival Records, a Guide to the Records of Immigrants Arriving at American Ports by Sail and Steam*, was published in 1988 by the G.P.C. Despite what the author calls 'dubious archival practices of the past', arrival records are shown to be 'surprisingly' complete, apart from those concerning the colonial and early federal periods. Mr Tepper takes the reader through all the intricacies of the creation, survival and location of such records, throughout the USA. Before the end of the eighteenth century no system of control had been introduced, being considered unnecessary. Only in Pennsylvania was any such recording carried out.

The book gives an outline of immigration in the colonial period, with information on the records of the time, and published material, pointing out the sad lack of co-ordination of the wealth of British archive material necessary to make any reasonable listing of emigration. It goes on to chart the beginning of *Federal Passenger Arrival Records*, the vast bulk of which date from January 1800. Not to be confused with Customs Passenger Lists, they were kept primarily at the port of Philadelphia and were known as 'Baggage Lists'. Philadelphia was some 20 years ahead of most of the rest of the country, and its lists deserve special study. The original baggage lists (1800–1819), with a few later examples, may be found in the Temple University/Balch Institute Center for Immigration Research in Philadelphia.

Customs Passenger Lists, on the other hand, were the result of legislation by Congress in 1819 to regulate the conveyance of immigrants from foreign ports, in an attempt to prevent overcrowding and thus improve conditions and lessen the chance of the dreaded 'ship fever' gaining hold. The Lists provide evidence that, over the years, nearly 20 million people arrived in the United States, between the enforcement of the Act and the turn of the century. This makes them the most important single body of arrival records in the country, and second only to the Federal Census Returns. Under the terms of the Act, masters of ships arriving from abroad had to hand over a manifest showing at least the following personal details: age; sex; occupation; country to which the immigrant 'belonged', and that of eventual destination, together with the date and circumstances of death should this have taken place during the crossing. The officials collecting these lists had to submit copies to the Secretary of State each quarter. He, in his turn, drew up a statement to be presented to Congress at each of its sessions.

The original lists, the copies, and the abstracts made from them, as well as transcripts of the quarterly returns prepared by the State Department, constitute that class of record known as Customer Passenger Lists, and are housed in the National Archives as Records of the U.S. Customs Service, Record Group 36.

By the middle of the nineteenth century, emigration from Europe to the United States had vastly increased. New York alone, in the year 1846, drew nearly 100,000 new arrivals, but in 1851 that number had almost trebled. The chief cause of this massive rise was of course the Irish Famine, which gave rise to a classic example of large-scale emigration. Mr Tepper's book includes a section on the emigration patterns of various communities including the Irish and the results of such an exodus.

The 1819 Act was hopelessly out of date by the 1840s; new Acts were brought in in 1847/8, and in 1855. These were ambitious but still remained ineffectual, owing to loopholes in their wording. No restrictions were placed on immigration until 1875 when criminals (but not those found guilty of political crimes) and prostitutes were barred by Congress. Until then any restrictions had been imposed at State level. This practice was declared unconstitutional in 1876 and, finally, on 3rd August 1882, federal immigration legislation was passed, placing control in the hands of the Treasury Department, which resulted in the appointment of a Superintendent of Immigration in 1891.

Apart from being a marked improvement on its predecessors, the 1882 Act required further information to be included on the manifests presented by ships' masters. For cabin passengers this was now: name; age; sex; occupation; country of birth, and intended destination or location. This was much more informative than previous listings, which stated only the country to which passengers 'belonged', not that of birth, and port of entry, not intended place of residence in North America.

A further Act of 1903 added a section stating the new arrival's race, as well as enlarging the definition of undesirable aliens, which now included such classes as epileptics, anarchists, professional beggars, previous deportees and those suffering recurring fits of lunacy.

In June 1906, after the passing of a Naturalization Act and the setting up of a Bureau of Immigration and Naturalization, it was decided that manifests were to carry a description of passengers, and list actual birthplaces; and, in 1907, that the name and address of the nearest relative still living in the old country should be given.

Thus by 1909, says Mr Tepper, the emigrant would be detailed in a list which might consist of up to 27 items, ranging from the usual name and age, to more practical and personal information, such as the state of the newcomer's health, mind and pocket book!

These Immigration Passenger Lists form a source of information in the National Archives, second only to Customs Passenger Lists, and have the classification Record Group 85, Records of the Immigration and Naturalization Service. Philadelphia once again has the earliest (1883) while those of the other ports date, on average, from the 1890s. Some ports kept separate lists of immigrants and American nationals returning home to the States.

Apart from the Atlantic and Gulf Coast ports, the Pacific ports and arrivals via various Canadian ports are included.

American Passenger Arrival Records has sections on the whereabouts of both the originals and copies on microfilm of Customer Passenger Lists. The majority of Immigrant Passenger Lists exist only in microfilm form, the originals having been deliberately destroyed by the Immigration and Naturalization Service after being filmed.

Table I shows the existence and years covered of originals, copies or abstracts, and of State Department Transcripts, and whether they are available on National Archive microfilm, from Alexandria Va. to Yarmouth Me., all relating to Customer Passenger Lists. A second table, this time of Immigrant Passenger Lists, gives lists and indexes of ports and districts from Apalachicola Fl. to West Palm Beach Fl. Throughout the book all classes of passenger arrival records are dealt with port by port, and location by location.

Naturalization Records

Researchers interested in establishing where, when, and indeed if, their ancestors became naturalized United States citizens should consult John J. Newman's booklet, *American Naturalization Processes and Procedures 1790–1985*, published by the Family History Section of Indiana Historical Society, 1985, which takes the reader through the steps involved. One must realize, though, that by no means all alien residents became naturalized citizens. Depending on the constitution of individual states, it was not necessarily essential so to do in order to vote, for example, or to own land.

Congress passed a series of acts from 1790 onwards granting courts powers of naturalization. These had differing names from state to state, but all were federal courts. In 1908 the Department of Labor began issuing *A Directory of Courts having Jurisdiction in Naturalization Proceedings*, listing them alphabetically by state. The 1963 edition, issued by the Department of Justice, lists the degree of activity, if any, of courts as regards naturalization.

In 1941–2 most states participated in the Works Projects Administration (WPA) effort, sponsored by the Department of Justice, which made copies of naturalization records created before 27 September 1906. The copies went to Washington where inventories were to be made. These are complete for Maine, Massachusetts, New Hampshire, Rhode Island and New York

City, and are in the National Archives' Record Group 85; other states are only partially complete. The Project finished in July 1942 and its work was deposited in state archives.

Microfilms of a number of records from courts nationwide have been filmed by the Genealogical Society of Utah. For original records after 1906 try the local court, or file No. G–641 with the Immigration and Naturalization Service, 425 1 Street NW, Washington DC 20536, where a fee will be charged. For naturalization files 1906–56, the office where the alien lived should be approached. Some states are transferring naturalization records from state and local courts to state archives and repositories.

Census Records

For a comprehensive account of American census schedules from 1790 onwards, consult Val D. Greenwood's *The Researcher's Guide to American Genealogy*, second edition, 1990, Baltimore, Genealogical Publishing Company, Inc. The earliest census portions which survive have been indexed and published under the title *Heads of Families at the First Census of the United States Taken in the Year 1790*, which is to be found in libraries throughout the country. A census has been taken every decade since, the latest one to come into the public domain being that of 1910.

All schedules (or returns) from 1800 to 1900, and 1900 and 1910 still extant, may be searched in the National Archives' copies. Tragically, the 1890 census was mostly destroyed by fire in 1921, only fragments surviving. These have been filmed (N407) and there is also an index to names (microcopy No. M496). Schedules 1800–1830 have been photostated and the copies bound; those of 1840–1880 have been microfilmed by the Census Bureau, as have those for 1900–1940. All those available to the public (that is, over 72 years old) are on microfilm at the LDS Family History Library, and sections are on film at other libraries, such as Washington State University at Pullman. 1790 to 1910 survivors can be obtained on interlibrary loan, or direct from the National Archives Microfilm Rental Program.

Similar to censuses are the Mortality Schedules, which begin with the 1850 census and give information on persons who had died during the census year. Mortality schedules exist for 1850 through 1880, and for the limited census of 1885. Unfortunately they give details for only one year in a decade or, theoretically, 13 per cent of the deaths, but in fact they fall far short of that, possibly as much as 40 per cent below for 1850–70. Information normally consists of: name, age, sex, state of birth, month of death and cause of death. Those for 1880 and 1885 also state birthplace of the deceased's parents, but not their names. The easiest way to research mortality schedules is through the Census Microfilm Rental Program; major holdings of originals are those of the National Archives, the Mormon Church's Family History Library and the Daughters of the American Revolution.

The Records of the Library of the Church of Jesus Christ of Latter-day Saints

We, in Britain, tend to think of the genealogical activities of the LDS as a basically American source of help for the family history researcher, and of the Saints, or Mormons as they are also called, as an American denomination. An article in *Family Tree Magazine*, Volume 5, Number 9, July 1989, by Gillian Smith, herself a Church member, proves otherwise.

As long ago as 1837 Heber C. Kimball, accompanied by six other missionaries from Joseph Smith's Church in America, landed at Liverpool to preach the gospel. Ten days later Kimball baptised nine people in the Ribble at Preston, Lancashire. In 1840 Wilford Woodruff reached, then went on into, the Midlands, and within eight months had baptised a further 1,800 converts. In the July of 1840, John Taylor went to Ireland where he too made many converts to the Church. In ten years about 35,000 people in Britain and Ireland had become Church members and, by the mid-1850s, there were more Mormons in Britain than in Salt Lake City, the Church's headquarters.

Emigration to Salt Lake City was encouraged, and a Perpetual Emigration System offered a family passage to America for only £10. Between 1840 and 1880, some 100,000 Britons left to join the Church in America. The Mormons' Family History Library (formerly the Genealogical Library) was founded in 1894 with the express purpose of gathering records, and helping Church members to make family trees.

Filming of all types of registers and records has been in progress since the 1950s, and there are currently 28 people engaged in so doing in Britain's record offices, museums and churches. To ensure preservation of records the Church stores them in an vault, safe against the ravages of time, weather and nuclear attack, in the Wasatch Mountains, near Salt Lake City.

In the Library, there is a complete floor of British and Irish records. In Britain itself, several chapels have Family History Centers, the next best thing actually to being in Salt Lake City to do research. The bulk of the holdings are on microfiche, but there are also books in micro-form, and films may be obtained on loan from the United States, for use at the Center nearest to the researcher's home. Centers offer the use of a film on how to carry out research, and the chapel librarian will show or loan it to interested family history societies.

Although, as the following description will show, the Mormon Church is now a world-wide institution, its roots remain firmly in America, so its holdings have been dealt with here in the American section to avoid duplication. Researchers interested in using the Church's facilities in their own countries should, of course, contact the Family History Center nearest to their own home.

The main Church Library, the Family History Library, is situated at 35 North West Temple Street, Salt Lake City, Utah 84150 (telephone (801) 240 2331). The new genealogical library was dedicated in October 1985, occupying five floors of holdings, with possible extension to three more storeys. It now constitutes the world's largest collection of genealogical records, open to the general public at no charge. The following is merely an outline of its major holdings:

Microfilms: 1,600,000 reels; equivalent to 6 million volumes of 300 pages.

Printed books and Manuscripts: around 200,000.

Names on Record: more than 2,000,000,000 with 8,000,000 families appearing on Family Group Record Forms.

Monthly Acquisitions: about 5,000 rolls of film and 1,000 books.

The International Genealogical Index (formerly the Computer File Index or C.F.I.) a data base of 121,000,000 names, to which are added a further 7,000,000 or so annually.

There is seating for 963 researchers, and the Library welcomes some 2,800 visitors each day!

In 44 countries all over the world, the Church has more than 1,200 libraries, and more than 1,300 Family History Centers.

The Church's main resources

The Family History Library Catalog (FHLC) which lists and describes holdings and their numbers, necessary to find or order records.

The FHLC is held on microfiche at Family History Centers.

The Family Registry is an index of some 215,000 persons and families who are willing to participate in sharing information. One may register one's own family. The index is available on microfiche at most Centers.

The Ancestral File is an ever-developing database which helps families to share information; one should send copies of one's tree to the Family History Department, Ancestral File Operations Unit, 50 East North Temple Street, Salt Lake City, Utah 84150.

The Personal Ancestral File is a software program designed for home computers, for the storage and arrangement of personal findings, and it will print out charts and records. At present it is only available in MS-DOS and Apple II formats.

The International Genealogical Index, or IGI, is described in great detail in the Church's leaflets 'Research Outline: International Genealogical Index (on microfiche)', 1988, and 'Research Outline: Finding an IGI Source', both of which are available from Family History Centers.

The IGI is used by researchers all over the world, and is of particular use to those who are not able to view original records for themselves. It can be time-saving both in avoidance of duplication of research, and in providing a ready source of information and establishing where a concentration of a particular surname occurs. The Church does, however, issue a warning as to the likelihood of errors, and stresses that the IGI 'is not an index to all of the records in our collection nor all of those records in the British Isles' or any other country come to that. As with anything undertaken by human hands, particularly one in which a large number of persons are involved, there are plenty of mistakes in the compilation of the IGI, in addition to which is the fact that whether or not a particular set of records has been filmed depends largely on the attitude of the incumbent towards the Church's genealogical work, and the conditions of the records themselves. Thus a considerable number of parishes are not included on the IGI. These comments in no way detract from the great achievement which the IGI and other such files and indexes undoubtedly represent, and are merely a reminder that they are a guide to sources, not sources in their own right, a fact which should be kept in mind when using them.

The IGI, with all its strengths and weaknesses, is a data base of some 121,000,000 names, all of them deceased persons. New editions appear in microfiche form every few years, the latest edition having been produced in 1988.

The information contained dates mainly from between the beginning of the sixteenth century and 1875, and consists of names of individuals with information concerning their birth and/or christening, marriage and Church temple ordinance. There is a reference number beside each entry so that the original source, with possible additional information, may be traced.

The names on the IGI come from three main sources. The majority are hand-copied and put onto computer by volunteers, from both civil and church records. These are chiefly birth, christening and marriage records, but not normally those of death or burial. This means that there is even more need to check the original source wherever possible as the 'perfect ancestor' may not have lived long after his christening. It should also be pointed out that not every event is to be found for every individual who appears on a fiche. Secondly, forms sent in by Church members, mostly since 1969, have the name taken from them and inserted into the IGI; and, thirdly, membership records for deceased Church members and certain temple records are also fed into it. If persons named in other records have no date or place of birth or marriage, however, they will not be included on the IGI, but in a Family Entry System which is as yet unindexed.

The IGI may be found on microfiche, not only at Salt Lake City but in Family History Centers world-wide, also in record offices and archives, libraries and family history society collections. It is possible for groups or individuals to purchase either fiches or printed copies for a small fee. Staff will conduct searches for a small charge, on receipt of a request form available from the Centers.

The names appear on the microfiche under the place in which the event took place, initially under country, then by state or county, then by surname. The nine Irish microfiches, however, are arranged under surname, not by county. If more than one person or event is listed under identical names, then entries appear in chronological order. Be prepared to look for alternative spellings of surnames; there is sometimes a 'See also' entry by certain names. With Irish surnames it is worth looking for the required name both with and without a 'Mac' or 'O' prefix.

The LDS produce a type of workbook entitled *A Guide to the*

Research: Genealogical Library of the Church of Jesus Christ of Latter-day Saints (1985). This gives opening hours, Library rules and regulations, and aims to help answer the five basic questions researchers are likely to ask: 'What do I know about my family?; What do I want to learn about my family?; What records does the Library have?; Where do I find a record?; What do I do next?.'

Major Irish holdings in the Family History Library and its satellites

For up-to-the-minute details of current holdings, either visit a Family History Center nearby, and search the 'Locality' section of the Family History Library Catalog, or order a copy of the Catalog for Ireland on microfiche; the 1989 price was $1.35. According to the British Correspondent in August 1989, 'not much in the way of primary sources are coming out of Ireland presently', however.

The LDS leaflet 'Basic Guide to Irish Genealogical Research' (1984) lists the 'basic but major' sources held in Salt Lake City as:

Civil Registration: Indexes from 1864 to 1958 of Births, Marriages and Deaths.
The actual entries 1864 to March 1881, 1900 to 1913, 1930 to 1955
Northern Ireland: Births 1922 to 1959.
Marriage entries, all Ireland: 1864 to 1870.
Protestant marriages with indexes: 1845 to 1863.
Northern Ireland Marriages: 1925 to 1959.
Death entries: 1864 to 1870.
Northern Ireland death entries: 1922 to 1959.

Census Returns: Microfilm of survivors, being portions of censuses for 1821, 1831, 1841 and 1851.

Tithe Applotment Books: 1823 to 1838, with Householders' Index to all counties.

Griffith's or Primary Valuation: 1848–1864; the copies are completely indexed.

Old Age Pension Claims (according to the Old Age Pension Act of 1908): claims held for Northern Ireland only.

Land Records: 1708 until the present day. One index is composed of vendors of land, another of land under its name, county by county; such records include transactions, marriage settlements, mortgages, wills and deeds.

The Purpose of Mormon Research into Family History

The Church's leaflet 'Family History Library' (1988) explains how the Genealogical Society of Utah founded a Family History Library in 1894, in line with its commitment towards preserving all records throughout the world. Its work has been financed by the Church of Jesus Christ of Latter-day Saints since the end of the last war. Today specialists are engaged on the Church's behalf in photography, archive administration, and the preservation and conservation of documents.

Mormons believe above all in the sanctity of family life, the sacraments known as 'ordinances' being of supreme importance. As many of our ancestors were not able to be baptised 'by proper authority', temples have been built wherein members of the Church may receive sacred ordinances on their behalf: the ancestors may then accept or not accept the ordinances, as they see fit. The leaflet invites 'our friends of all faiths and creeds to use these resources to learn about their own ancestors.' It would be a mistake not to take advantage of the wonderful generosity, enthusiasm and efficiency of the Church of Jesus Christ of Latter-day Saints.

The Irish in America

As we have already seen, many Irishmen, both Catholic and Protestant, soon settled down and made their mark on the American scene, or at least paved the way for their sons or grandsons to do so.

The great mass of immigrants, however, arrived as country people suddenly faced with the choice of finding work in a big city, or of starving in the New World instead of the Old. In their search for cheaper housing, Irish labourers had to take whatever they could afford and this drove them to the most run-down areas of town, where they were resented by the existing residents who objected to their making slums of districts which were squalid enough to begin with. The new arrivals, poor, uneducated, in a low state of health, and with everything to learn, were at the very bottom of the urban pile in cities such as New York (particularly in Brooklyn and Manhattan), Boston and Philadelphia. Not surprisingly, infant mortality was high and, in Boston in the 1850s, the average age at death was about 22.

Gradually, though, the Irish managed to drag themselves off the lowest rung of the social ladder, their places soon being taken by later arrivals, many of whom could not even speak English. By the time of the Civil War (1861 to 1865) 38 Union regiments had the word 'Irish' as part of their title, and by the end of the century Irish attempts at gentility and respectability had become the butt of American cartoonists who found them amusingly pretentious.

It was at this period that the differences became very marked between the Protestant Irish, of Scots origin, who were achieving considerable respectability, and the Catholic Irish, who remained lower on the scale of social acceptability. Nowadays, the term 'Irish' is generally reserved for Catholics in the United States, and is not usually applied to Presbyterians of Scots-Irish descent.

American aid to Ireland during the Famine

According to Cassell's *Illustrated History of England*, written when the Victorian era had just drawn to a close, the help which Americans sent to the Irish famine victims was 'on a scale unparalleled in history'. It goes on to describe meetings in Philadelphia, Washington, New York, and other cities, where great interest and anxiety were shown.

Railway companies sent all packages which were marked 'Ireland' free of charge, and public carriers also declined a fee. Warships sailed to Ireland laden with food, in all a hundred shipments, on which the British Government paid the freight charges which ran to £33,000. A quantity of nearly 10,000 tons, worth about £100,000, was sent, plus £16,000 in cash, 642 packages of clothing, and private money sent home to their families by individuals; altogether a colossal undertaking. The sums sent by emigrants in America to Ireland were printed by order of Parliament: (1848) £460,180; (1849) £540,619; (1850) £957,087; (1851) £990,811.

The Americans have shown themselves equally generous on many occasions since then, notably during World War II, with food and clothing parcels, and recently to Third World countries. Unnecessary, but very touching nevertheless, was the arrival of parcels to Britain during the fuel crisis of 1974! This trait, probably the Americans' most lovable characteristic, could well have had its origins in the selflessness shown to others in distress by the Irish during their own periods of crisis.

93

2. Canada; the Public Archives in Ottawa

In a country as new and as vast as Canada (it is second in area only to the USSR) the authorities have always encouraged immigration, without, however, curbing the immigrant's pride and awareness of his ancestral culture.

A good starting-place in trying to trace one's first Canadian ancestor, if he was a comparatively early arrival, is the 1851 Census, which is kept in the Dominion's Public Archives, 395 Wellington Street, Ottawa, Ontario K1A ON3 (telephone 613 995 5138).

Founded in 1872, the Archives produce a comprehensive booklet, *Tracing Your Ancestors in Canada*, which is updated periodically. It lists the principal Provincial Archives, with their own addresses and telephone numbers, as well as describing its own holdings. The Public Archives, however, cannot offer a research service, information being restricted to advice concerning source material held, and its usefulness to the researcher. There is available, however, a list of researchers willing to undertake commissions for a fee.

Principal Canadian records of interest to the family historian are:

Census Records and Voters' Lists.
Civil Registration and Church Records.
Land and Estate Claims and Papers.
Military and Naval Records, plus Empire Loyalist Sources.
Naturalization and Citizenship Records.

Immigration records held by the Public Archives

These records give very little information about those persons arriving in Canada prior to 1865 as, until that year, ships' captains were not legally obliged to keep detailed passenger lists. The few surviving earlier lists usually name groups of immigrants, paid for by a sponsor, and normally from Britain. They form part of the Colonial Office Series 384, with an index 1817 to 1831, on microfilm (reel C 4252). The microfilms show name, former residence, occupation and date of entry.

The Canadian Public Archives hold microfilms of these manifests (that is, invoices of what the ship was carrying, drawn up for customs clearance) for arrivals at the following ports:

Quebec City 1865–1908
Halifax, N.S. 1880–1908
St John, N.S. 1900–1908
Victoria, B.C. 1905–1908
Vancouver 1905–1908
and via the ports of Baltimore, Boston, New York, Portland,
   and Philadelphia: 1905–1908

Manifests show the passenger's:
Name, Age, Occupation, and intended destination.
It is necessary to know the exact date and port of arrival, plus, of
course, the name of the ship on which the ancestor reached
Canada. A consolidated indexing system of the manifests should be
completed by 1988.

For those immigrants arriving after 1908, enquiries should be
made to the Records of Entry Unit, Canada Employment and
Immigration Commission, Place du Portage, Phase IV, Hull,
Quebec KA OJP.

It should be noted that post-1910 records may be consulted only
with the permission of the immigrant concerned, or with proof of
his or her death.

The Commission also holds lists of post-1918 immigration via
the United States, the researching of which requires a knowledge
of the point of entry to Canada, and the approximate date of
arrival. Lists of emigrants from Canada to the United States were
not kept.

Canada province by province

As with the United States and the states which make up Australia,
the Canadian provinces vary considerably as regards their order of
settlement, and, of course, the periods which their records cover.

The oldest Canadian province is Ontario, which still demonstrates its essential Britishness by holding Orange Day parades on
12th July, the anniversary of the Battle of the Boyne, 1690, when
the supporters of the Catholic James II were routed by those of
Protestant William III.

Newfoundland, together with the other Maritime (or Atlantic)
Provinces – New Brunswick, Nova Scotia, and Prince Edward
Island – has a noticeably Celtic background, which is evident in
distinctive speech patterns, similar to Irish ones, and the use of
Irish idioms. The folksongs, too, are reminiscent of 'home',

'Newfie' jokes bear a strong resemblance to Irish ones, and the inhabitants celebrate both St Patrick's Day and Orange Day.

British Columbia is known all over North America for its strong ties with Britain, down to Marks and Spencer, double-decker red buses, 4 o'clock tea-time and bagpipe playing!

Next in seniority are Manitoba and Saskatchewan, with Alberta being the youngest province.

During the course of the nineteenth and twentieth centuries, Vital Statistics Acts were passed in turn by the individual provinces in order to start Civil Registration; records vary, therefore, from one to another.

Church records, on average, date from the last century, although, once again, this varies according to the place under consideration. Both civil and church records are kept in the provincial capitals.

An Irish-Canadian Cultural Association has been formed to promote Irish culture, language, literature and arts. It aims to 'be a source of guidance to anyone wishing to trace their genealogy' and states that eastern Canada is 'rich with' people of Irish descent. A Canadian-Irish Harmony Festival has been arranged, it is hoped on an annual basis.

In 1986 the Festival lasted three days and attracted 18,000 visitors. Details are available from Dave Furlotte, PO Box 1151, Dalhousie, N.B., E0K 1BO, Canada, the writer of a letter published to promote the Cultural Association and its activities in the St Patrick's Day edition of *Ireland's Own* magazine 1987.

For a full description of Canadian sources with their dates and locations, see Angus Baxter's *In Search of Your Canadian Roots* (Genealogical Publishing Co. Inc., Baltimore 1989).

This comprehensive book, one of a series by Mr Baxter, highlights purely Canadian sources of records, generated by new arrivals over the years of the country's colonization. Among those included are English, Irish, Scottish, German, Huguenot, Jewish and Ukrainian immigrants, with particular mention of the National Archives and the Mormon Church's holdings relating to Canada.

At a more local level, the author takes Canadian family historians through each of the Provinces and the Yukon and Northwest Territories, listing the major records held by each, together with lists of archives, libraries and societies.

3. Australia

When in search of that first emigrant ancestor's arrival in Australia, it is essential to bear in mind that lists of arrivals are kept in the relevant state record office; there is no central Australian repository for such sources, so all investigation must be carried out at state level.

To find an individual a certain amount of basic information is needed:

Name; Port of Entry; Name of Vessel; Date of Arrival in Australia.

People must be searched for as individuals, not as part of a family unit for, in many cases, children were not always listed separately from their parents, and one may have to rely on their turning up in later entries in their own right. It is essential then, to have as much information as one possibly can, including any distinguishing features which might serve to differentiate between emigrants of the same name.

The information usually to be found on shipping lists consists of: Name of the Ship and her master; Port of Departure; the Date of Arrival in Australia; and personal details of passengers, such as Name; Age; Sex; Country of Birth, including the Place; and Occupation.

It is useful to list here the various categories of passenger, as listed by the shipping companies:

Free: fare paid by the government.

Assisted: fare partly paid.

Unassisted: the passenger paid his own way.

Bounty: fare paid by an agent who would receive a fee from the government.

Nominated or Remitted: fare paid by someone already in the new country.

Once the first arrival has been traced, Australian civil records (apart from the Census) you will find to be especially good, as many immigrants arrived under some type of official scheme, ranging from transportation to the £10 assisted passage.

Sources documenting life after arrival

Church records in Australia form a useful source of information for an ancestor living before the start of Civil Registration. Most registers start in the early nineteenth century, and they are usually kept at the office of the Registrar-General of the state concerned.

Australian census returns are deliberately destroyed after the information they contain has been extracted for statistical purposes. They are not, therefore, looked on by the authorities as a source of social or family history, and Australian research is that much the poorer for it. Some early survivors do exist, however, that of New South Wales for 1828 being particularly interesting. It lists more than 35,000 inhabitants, giving their:

Age; Trade; Residence whether living in or outside New South Wales; Land and Stock held; Name of Ship in which arrived in Australia.

What returns exist for New South Wales are held in the Mitchell Library in Sydney. It is possible to find out the name of one's ancestor's ship from the census if one is lucky enough to find the right return, and then go on to search the passenger lists in the Library. Tasmania, too, has a useful 1842 census which is in the Hobart Archives.

Civil Registration, although carried out on a regional basis, is similar in all states, and much more informative than its counterpart in either Ireland or Britain. Registration started at different dates in different states, for instance in Victoria in 1853 and in New South Wales in 1856, but details remain equally helpful.

Birth certificates give the birthplace of the father, the date and place of the parents' marriage, the maiden surname of the mother, and her age and birthplace, as well as details of all other children, alive or dead. Marriage certificates give the maiden surname of the mother, and death certificates burial details, the name and occupation of the deceased's father, and the maiden surname of the mother, plus the number of years resident in Australia. Also given are details of spouse, marriage, and any children of the marriage. All this is in addition to the details which one would find on British certificates.

Printed material
Publications such as the *New South Wales Government Gazette* from 1832 to 1886 give extensive details of land grants, probates, and other information of value to family historians.

The world's largest society of family historians, the Australian Society of Genealogists, with a membership of over 11,000, is involved in many projects, not the least of which is a transcription of the inscriptions on the gravestones of the enormous Rookwood Cemetery, near Sydney, which has more than a million graves, and which is being put onto microfilm. The Australian Society of Archivists, PO Box 83, O'Connor, ACT 2601, issues *Our Heritage: A Directory to Archives and Manuscript Repositories in Australia*, which describes principal holdings and their whereabouts, and is available from the Society's Treasurer, at the above address.

Nick Vine Hall in *Tracing your Ancestors in Australia*, the most up-to-date and comprehensive book on the subject, includes an Appendix, 'Published Family Histories', which lists all those pedigrees included in the records of the Australian Society of Genealogists.

Australia – The Early Years, compiled from reports in the *Derry Journal*, and published by the Genealogy Centre, 10 Bishop Street, Londonderry BT48 6PW, provides documentary evidence of the part played by Irish emigrants in the early settlement of Australia. The *Derry Journal* first appeared in June 1772, well before the landing of the historic First Fleet in 1788. *Australia – The Early Years*, however, deals with the period 1838–1846, which, of course, includes Ireland's worst famine years. At this period, the journal was called the *Londonderry Journal and Donegal and Tyrone Advertiser*, and appeared weekly. It had a 4-page format, and cost 4½d. The contents consisted of international and colonial news of interest to British readers in general, Irish news, local events and happenings, views, and letters. Most important of all, for our purposes, was page 3, containing lists of shipping arriving and leaving the port of Derry, together with Births, Deaths and Marriages, and details of steamer services to Liverpool and Glasgow, as well as crossings to North America and as far as Australia.

Naturally, Australia is mentioned in a variety of articles and lists, from the transportation of convicts and the emigration of free Ulstermen to the settlement and exploration of the new country itself. Convicts awaiting transportation were imprisoned in the gaol in the very street where the Genealogy Centre now stands.

Apart from the convicts, between 1837 and 1838 about 1,000 Ulster people took advantage of a Government-assisted scheme to settle in and around Sydney. Among them were men destined to help shape the future of their new homeland, notably Robert Torrens in South Australia, and George Fletcher Moore in Western Australia.

Finally, a rather sad comment from a leading Australian family historian, Mrs K. R. Pullman, who says that there is a 'great need for up-to-date information on what records are coming forward'. Apparently, it is 'hard to get Irish researchers to reply in what we regard as a reasonable time', for 'some do not even reply to initial enquiries.'

4. New Zealand

The earliest immigration records, those of the New Zealand Company, which are indexed and housed in the New Zealand Archives, PO Box 6162, Te Aro, Wellington, deal with Wellington, Nelson, New Plymouth and Otago, all for the years 1840 to 1850.

The information that they contain consists of: Name, Age, Occupation, Age of Wife and Ages and Sexes of any Children. Between 1853 and 1876, New Zealand was governed at provincial level, therefore sources and dates differ between the provinces.

Useful local sources include:

Auckland: Registers of persons applying for passage 1859 to 1872 (remember that these applications were not automatically granted); Shipping lists 1882 to 1887, including Names of Crew, and of both assisted and unassisted passengers.

Canterbury: Embarkation registers for assisted passengers 1855 to 1883 (indexed 1855 to 1870).

Hawkes Bay and Southland: Both have lists of a few payments made for passage.

Nelson: A few passenger lists 1853 to 1876.

Otago: List of debtors owing money to the provincial government for passages 1848 to 1869 (indexed).

Wellington: A few passenger lists 1853 to 1876; Shipping lists 1857 to 1910, giving Names of Crew and both assisted and unassisted passengers.

Tasmania (formerly Van Dieman's Land): Tasmania played an important role in receiving immigrants to New Zealand in the early years of its colonization. The Archives Office, at 91, Murray Street, Hobart 7000 holds much documentary material concerning New Zealand. For details see *Guide to the Public Records of Tasmania* (Section Four, Free Immigration) by Ian Pearce and Clare Cowling, available from the Hobart Archives.

Between 1871 and 1881 an Agent General operated in London, whose responsibility it was to control emigration to New Zealand.

Church records
These records are still held by the parish concerned, regardless of denomination. The early ones date back to at least the 1820s. However, permission is needed from the custodian before any register may be consulted.

Some early Anglican registers are available on microfilm. A survey conducted in 1966 showed New Zealanders to be 33.7% Church of England, followed by 21.8% Presbyterian, and 15.9% Roman Catholic, thus reflecting the denominations of the various nations which went to make up New Zealand, in their proportions.

The Census
Although there are a few early survivors – the Census in New Zealand having started as early as 1801 – which give Name, Age, Sex and Occupation, and are kept in the National Archives, New Zealand pursues the same policy towards censuses as Australia in that they are destroyed after use. The next best thing is the Militia Returns for the 1840s, which list all able-bodied men in Wellington. The Colonial Office's 'Blue Books' name civil servants and criminals together!

Civil Registration
The registration of Europeans was not compulsory in New Zealand until 1848, and then only for births and deaths. Marriages were not included by law until 1855.

Certificates may be seen at the office where the event was originally registered, and the actual entry may be seen and copied by hand, a cheaper method than buying certified copies. A maximum of 3 'sightings' per person is permitted.

Birth certificates issued after 1876 are more full than their predecessors, and Form RG 100, the full certificate, has the date and place of the parents' marriage typed on the back.

Marriage certificates are more full after 1880. Two types of certificate were in use, Form RG 118 being the full one.

Death certificates after 1876 are helpful in that they give the place of birth, particularly useful when in search of that first arrival. They also give place of burial, and the name of parents, with the mother's maiden name.

Wills

These are kept in the High Court (formerly known as the Supreme Court) nearest to the last place of residence of the deceased. There is unfortunately no central index to wills in New Zealand but, if they were lodged with the Public Trust before the mid-1950s, they would have been probated in Wellington High Court, regardless of where death took place. To trace a will, the deceased's full name and date of death are essential.

The New Zealand Society of Genealogists is busy transcribing gravestones. The inscriptions from more than 700 cemeteries have been put on microfilm and forwarded to the Mormon Church's Genealogical Library in Salt Lake City for distribution. The Society's journal is *The New Zealand Genealogist*, and journals are exchanged with other family history societies world-wide. The main Society includes a smaller Irish Society within its ranks.

An influx of emigrants from Australia to New Zealand at the beginning of the present century, and during the 1930s, brought more Irish blood, and with it the need for New Zealanders to do research in Australian archives, as well as in their own and British ones.

Libraries in New Zealand which are particularly strong in Irish and British material are the Alexander Turnbull Library, PO Box 12349, Wellington North, and Auckland Public Library, which has much of the holdings from the Public Record Offices of both Ireland and Northern Ireland on microfilm.

South Africa

Repositories

South African archive material is housed at provincial level in the various National Archive Depots: for Cape Province, which is the oldest, dating from 1876, Natal, the Free State and Transvaal, situated respectively in Cape Town, Pietermaritzburg, Bloemfontein and Pretoria, with a Central Depot in Pretoria which handles material generated since 1910.

In addition to the usual documentary sources, each Depot has computer output terminals which give the researcher access to material held in the other Depots, and in certain other repositories. Archive Depots are open free to the public by admission ticket obtained in advance. While advice on sources held is given, there is no search service.

The Division for Biographical and Genealogical Research of the Human Sciences Research Council, Pretoria, offers an important source of help and guidance; they are always willing to advise, although they do not actually undertake research commissions. They hold both published and unpublished material, and very useful microfilms, as well as assisting in the publication of works on family history.

Deeds Registries, situated in Bloemfontein, Cape Town, Johannesburg, Kimberley, King William's Town, Pietermaritzburg, Pretoria and Vryburg, provide much useful information, due to the necessity for all freehold and sectional title of fixed property to be registered before the title is complete; the details required include the full names and dates of birth of the owners of the property in question.

As elsewhere, particularly in countries far away from original sources such as early parish registers, the IGI and the rest of the contents of Branch Genealogical Libraries of the Church of Jesus of Latter-day Saints play an important role. These are situated in Johannesburg, Durban and Cape Town.

Civil Registration

In South Africa Civil Registration is handled centrally by the Registry of Births, Marriages and Deaths, Ministry of Home Affairs, Pvt. Bag X 114, Pretoria 0001. Unfortunately there are no indexes available for public use.

Civil Registration began at different dates for the various components of South Africa, as follows:

	Births	Marriages	Deaths
Cape	1895	1700	1895
Natal	1868	1845	1888
Transvaal	1901	1870	1901
Orange Free State	1903	1848	1903

There are two types of certificate, the abridged and the full: the latter should, of course, be used by family historians. Because certificates are accepted in South African courts of law as prime evidence, they are likely to be more accurate than those issued in other countries, although, of course, errors do creep in.

There is no charge for certificates, but formal application must be made, preferably on the Registry's own forms. Postal requests, though, may be accepted if they give all the relevant information. It is possible to collect certificates from the Registry, but the normal way is to have them sent through the post, allowing at least a month for them to arrive.

Census returns

The first Census taken in South Africa was that of Cape Colony in 1865, and many have been taken since. None survive, however, due to the government's policy, as in Australia and New Zealand, of destroying them after statistical information has been extracted.

The West Rand Family History Society, under the Chairmanship of Mr Mark Tapping, to whom I am indebted for the whole of my information on family history research in the Union of South Africa, has recently sent in a petition requesting the Minister responsible to reconsider this policy of destruction, but so far to no avail. The Society has not yet given up!

Church and chapel registers

There is no established church in South Africa, that is, no denomination has more prestige than another.

Until 1778 there was only one authorized church, the Dutch Reformed Church (Nederduitse Gereformeerde Kerk). Today this is the largest and most influential of the South African churches, followed by the Anglican Church of the Province of Southern Africa, and then the Methodist and Roman Catholic Churches.

English registers began with those records kept by military chaplains with the British forces of occupation, and date from 1795. They are held in the Guildhall Library, London, England, with the Bishop of London's records.

Dutch Reformed Church registers are extremely important owing to the fact that all church baptisms, marriages and burials were recorded in their pages from 1665 to 1778 and, in many areas, long afterwards. These registers are mainly kept in the Dutch Reformed Church's Archives in Cape Town, Bloemfontein, Pietermaritzburg and Pretoria. It is possible to obtain copies of entries, and all the earliest registers have been microfilmed and may be consulted elsewhere.

The registers of other churches are spread throughout the country, in archives, libraries, universities, church offices, and in private hands. Of these, the Church of the Province of Southern Africa is striving to trace and preserve all of its own early registers.

Wills

The office responsible for the acceptance of wills and the administration of deceased estates is that of the Master of the Supreme Court (usually known simply as the 'Master'). Masters' Offices are to be found in Bloemfontein, Cape Town, Grahamstown, Kimberley, Pietermaritzburg and Pretoria.

Original wills, and the even more important death notices, are kept by Masters' Offices in respect of more recent estates. All files of older estates have been passed to the various National Archive Depots, where they may be readily consulted. Deceased estates are indexed locally, and national computerized indexes, which have been compiled by the National Archives Service, are added to periodically.

Copies of documents in the Archives cost the copying fee only, but those in Masters' Offices cost about R 2, payable in local revenue stamps.

Family history societies in South Africa

The Genealogical Society of South Africa, PO Box 3057, Coetzenburg 7602, is in the process of reorganization, which means that its control is likely to be moved from Cape Town to the

Transvaal. However, it has branches nationwide which keep members up-to-date, and most are engaged in recording memorial inscriptions, with one member who is responsible for co-ordinating the results and passing them on to the National Archives so that they may be computerized and published. There are three volumes to date.

The Society's branches are in Cape Town, Port Elizabeth, Bloemfontein, Durban, Pietermaritzburg, Johannesburg and Pretoria.

THE ANCESTOR AT HOME: IRELAND

Sooner or later it is to be hoped that your ancestral trail will lead you to Ireland itself. Unlike England and Wales, and like Scotland, Ireland has no County Record Offices, the central depositories being the Public Record Offices in Dublin and Belfast. Unfortunately, documents and records may be distributed throughout the country, for instance in parishes, in solicitors' offices, in libraries and universities, and in private hands. The best places to start are the state record offices which, if they do not actually hold the records you need, may well have copies in one form or another, or at least be able to advise you of their whereabouts if, indeed, they exist.

Civil Registration

On 1st April 1845, the first stage of Civil Registration was introduced in Ireland; accordingly all *non*-Roman Catholic marriages had to be recorded. Although these did not represent a large proportion of Irish weddings, the entries filled 19 volumes from 1845 to 1863, in which year the Compulsory Registration Act was passed.

Full registration followed on 1st January 1864, over a quarter of a century later than in England and Wales (1837), Tasmania (1838), and well after New Zealand (1848) and Scotland (1855). Entries throughout the 1860s and 1870s are irregular, with plenty of omissions, particularly for births and deaths, perhaps as many as 10%. Tracing what should legally have been recorded may well turn out to be quite a hit-and-miss business. Not surprisingly, most problems occur in the Dublin and Cork areas, around the country's largest cities, which were undergoing rapid urbanization. Needless to say, many Irish people whose births were registered in Ireland had their marriages and deaths registered abroad.

All civil returns, for the whole of the country, made before

Partition in 1921, are with the Registrar General at the General Register Office in Dublin, as of course are those for the Republic since that year. Returns for the Six Counties of Ulster from 1922 onwards are with the Registrar General for Northern Ireland, Oxford House, 49–55 Chichester Street, Belfast, where Indexes for all-Ireland returns 1864–1922 are available for consultation. For the information contained on Irish civil registration certificates, see the following sections on Birth and Baptism, Marriage, and Death and Burial.

Census returns

Censuses have been taken in Ireland every ten years, starting in 1821, twenty years before the first one to list individuals was taken in England and Wales. The returns were carried out chiefly by members of the Irish Constabulary who, one presumes, were considered to have the necessary authority to persuade people to answer truthfully. As we have already seen, however, these gentlemen had neither the time nor the inclination to pursue social nonentities into the remotest parts of the country, in order to put their details on record for a government many miles away in Dublin.

Complete sets of the original enumerators' lists survive only for 1901 and 1911, the Censuses for the years 1861 to 1891 having been deliberately turned to pulp to help the war effort. Some, however, were copied into individual parish histories prior to 1922, and others are to be found in parish registers.

Returns were compiled under townlands, in rural areas, or under streets, in towns and villages. They consist of: Form A, which was filled in by the head of the household, and listed the names of all its members, with their ages, occupations, religion, and places of birth; and Forms N, B1, and B2, which were compiled by the enumerator himself, and made up summaries of each townland or street.

Apart from the 1901 and 1911 returns, some survive for 1821, 1831, 1841 and 1851, for parts of Antrim, Cavan, Co. Cork, Fermanagh, Galway, King's County (Offaly), Derry, Meath and Waterford.

In the Reading Room of the Irish Public Record Office is a detailed list of existing returns called 'Nineteenth-Century Census.'

Old age pension claims

When old age pensions were introduced in 1909, claims included those made by persons who had been born before the start of full civil registration in 1864, and were therefore not in possession of a birth certificate. In these cases searches were made of the Censuses in which claimants appeared, and the results were considered proof of age. The findings of these searches are recorded in the Public Record Office of Northern Ireland.

The Primary Valuation

This (also known as 'Griffith's Valuation') was made by the government on both land and property in order to enforce the terms of the Poor Law Act of 1838, by which each person who could afford to do so was obliged to help support the poor of his parish. The Primary Valuation, then, was an early rates system, and served to determine each person's liability to pay contributions for the upkeep of the local poor house. The initial rate payable was 6d in the £ and, naturally enough, contributors tended to belittle rather than exaggerate the value of their holdings.

Property valuation returns are particularly valuable in view of the nearly complete destruction of the Census returns, and show names of occupiers of land and buildings, the person from whom the land was leased, the amount of property held, and its estimated value.

The alternative name, Griffith's Valuation, comes from Sir Richard Griffith who compiled lists for the years 1848–1864, running to more than 200 volumes. Near-complete sets are in the National Library of Ireland, the Genealogical Office, and the PRO, which has a volume for each county.

Ordnance Survey Findings

In the early 1830s the Ordnance Survey began work on a series of maps designed to cover the whole of Ireland, on a scale of six inches to the mile. These maps duly appeared between 1835 and 1846, but minus all descriptive writing which had been carried out for each parish but found to be too cumbersome to include.

3 *Five completed Census return forms from the early 1900s (pp. 110–19)*

CENSUS

Two Examples of th

RETURN of the MEMBERS of this FAMILY and their VISITORS, BOARI

	NAME AND SURNAME.		RELATION to Head of Family.	RELIGIOUS PROFESSION.	EDUCATION.
Number.	*No Persons ABSENT on the Night of Sunday, April 2nd, to be entered here; EXCEPT those (not enumerated elsewhere) who may be out at WORK or TRAVELLING, &c., during that Night, and who RETURN HOME on MONDAY, APRIL 3RD.* *Subject to the above instruction, the Name of the Head of the Family should be written first; then the names of his Wife, Children, and other Relatives; then those of Visitors, Boarders, Servants, &c.*		State whether "Head of Family," or "Wife," "Son," "Daughter," or other Relative; "Visitor," "Boarder," "Servant," &c.	State here the particular Religion, or Religious Denomination, to which each person belongs. [Members of Protestant Denominations are requested not to describe themselves by the vague term "Protestant," but to enter the name of the Particular Church, Denomination, or Body to which they belong.]	State here whether b or she can "Rea and Write," ca "Read" only, o "Cannot Read."
	Christian Name.	Surname.			
	1.	2.	3.	4.	5.
1	Mathew	Schröder	Head of Family Father	Jew	Cannot read
2	Leah	Schröder	Daughter	Jewess	Read & write
3					
4					
5					
6					
7					
8					
9					
10					
11					
12					
13					
14					
15					

I hereby certify, as required by the Act 10 Edw. VII., and 1 Geo. V., cap. 11, that the foregoing Return is correct, according to the best of my knowledge and belief.

Michael M‘G___ Signature of Enumerator.

110

F IRELAND, 1911.

of filling up this Table are given on the other side.

FORM A.

ERVANTS, &c., who slept or abode in this House on the night of SUNDAY, the

ast Birthday) d SEX.	RANK, PROFESSION, OR OCCUPATION.	PARTICULARS AS TO MARRIAGE.					WHERE BORN.
				State for each Married Woman entered on this Schedule the number of :—			
Age opposite e :—the Ages in column 6, he Ages of in column 7. ats under one the age in as "under 1 " 1 month," aths," &c.	State the particular Rank, Profession, Trade, or other Employment of each person. Children or young persons attending a School, or receiving regular instruction at home, should be returned as *Scholars*. [No entry should be made in the case of wives, daughters, or other female relatives solely engaged in domestic duties at home.] Before filling this column you are requested to read the instructions on the other side.	Whether "Married," "Widower," "Widow," or "Single."	Completed years the present Marriage has lasted. If less than one year, write "under one."	Children born alive to present Marriage. If no children born alive, write "None" in column 11.		If in Ireland, state in what County or City; if elsewhere, state the name of the Country.
Ages of Females.				Total Children born alive.	Children still living.	
7.	8.	9.	10.	11.	12.	13.
	Hebrew Teacher	Widower				Russia
34		Single				Russia

I believe the foregoing to be a true Return.

Mathens Schreiter _____ Si,

111

CENSUS OF

FORM B. 1.—HOUSE

County,_____ Parliamentary Division, *St Patrick's* Poor Law Union, _____

Parliamentary Borough,} _____ City, *Dublin* Urban District,} _____ Town or Village

NOTE A—When a Townland or Street is situated in two Parliamentary Divisions, or in more than one District Electoral Division or Parish, or

HOUSES.

No. of House or Building (Col. 1)	Whether Built or Building (Col. 2)	State whether Private Dwelling, Public Building, School, Manufactory, Hotel, Poorhouse, Lodging-house, or shop, &c. (Col. 3)	Number of Out-offices and Farm-steadings as returned on Form B. 2. (Col. 4)	Is House Inhabited Yes or No (Col. 5)	WALLS (Col. 6)	ROOF (Col. 7)	ROOMS (Col. 8)	Windows in Front (Col. 9)	Total the Figures you have entered in columns 6, 7, 8, 9, and enter the Total for each House in this column (Col. 10)
1	Built	Private Dwelling	—	Yes	1	1	3	1	6
2	Do	Do	—	Yes	1	1	3	1	6
3	Do	Do	—	Yes	1	1	3	3	8
4	Do	Do	—	Yes	1	1	3	3	8
5	Do	Do	—	Yes	1	1	3	3	8
6	Do	Do	—	Yes	1	1	3	3	8
7	Do	Do	—	Yes	1	1	3	3	8
8	Do	Do	—	Yes	1	1	3	3	8
9	Do	Do	—	Yes	1	1	2	3	7
10	Do	Do	—	Yes	1	1	2	2	6
11	Do	Do	—	Yes	1	1	2	2	6
12	Do	Do	—	Yes	1	1	3	4	9
13	Do	Do	—	Yes	1	1	2	2	6
=	—	—	—	—	—	—	—	—	—
14	Built	Private Dwelling	—	Yes	1	1	2	3	7
15	Do	Do	—	Yes	1	1	2	3	7
20	Do	Do	—	Yes	1	1	2	2	6

NOTE B.—If one Room is occupied by more than one Family, the Names of the Heads of Families so occupying it should be bracketted together in

ELAND, 1901.

BUILDING RETURN.

Dublin District Electoral Division, _____ Townland, _____

Street, *St Kevins Parade and Wood Quay* Parish, *St Peters*

within and partly without a Parliamentary Borough, City, Urban District, Town, or Village, a *separate Return* should be made for each portion.

HOUSE. Col. 11	No. of distinct Families in each House. (Col 12)	Name of the Head of each Family residing in the House. (Col 13)	No. of Rooms occupied by each Family. (Col 14)	Total Number of Persons in each Family. (Col 15)	Date on which Form A was collected. (Col 16) 1901	Number of Persons in each Family who were sick on 31st March, 1901. (Col 17)	Name of the Landholder (if any) on whose Holding the House is situated, whether that name appears in column 13 or not. (Col 18)	No. on Form N. 1 of Houses on the Holding of a Landholder. (Col 19)
1	1	Patrick Bolger	6	6	April			
1	1	Falk Ginsberg	6	2	Do			
1	1	Yindle Myers	5	5	Do			
1	1	Sama Epstein	5	3	Do			
1	1	William Becker	5	7	Do			
1	1	Solomon Goldfoot	5	6	Do			
1	1	Mathew Shreider	5	5	Do			
1	1	David Besser	5	10	Do			
1	1	David Isaacson	4	5	Do			
1	1	Patrick Cahill	4	5	Do			
1	1	Joseph Flanagan	4	5	Do			
1	1	Jacob Green	5	10	Do			
1	2	Isac Herzog	3	2	Do			
-		Nathan Abiamovitz	2	3	Do			
1	1	Bernard Cohen	4	9	Do			
1	1	Lewis Harris	4	6	Do			
1	1	James Keenan	4	3	Do			

NB:— John Jones, Peter Murray, } and the figure 1 entered in Col. 14, opposite the middle of the bracket. See pattern Table in Instructions, page 9. [OVER

CENSUS OF

FORM B. 1.—HOUSE

County, *Of City of Dublin* Parliamentary Division, *St Patricks* Poor Law Union, *J*

Parliamentary Borough, } _____ City, *Dublin* Urban District, } _____ Town Village

Note A.—When a Townland or Street is situated in two Parliamentary Divisions, or in more than one District Electoral Division or Parish,

HOUSES.

No. of House	Whether Built or Building	State whether Private Dwelling, Public Building, School, Manufactory, Hotel, Public House, Lodging-house, or Shop, &c.	Number of Out-Offices and Farm-steadings as returned on Form B. 2.	Is House Inhabited? Yes or No as the case may be.	WALLS. If Walls are of Stone, Brick, or Concrete, enter the figure 1 in this column; if they are of Mud, Wood, or other perishable material, enter the figure 0.	ROOF. If Roof is of Slate, Iron, or Tiles, enter the figure 1 in this column; if it is of Thatch, Wood, or other perishable material, enter the figure 0.	ROOMS. Enter in this column— For each House with 1 Room (the figure 1 only) For House with 2, 3, or 4 rooms 2 5 or 6 3 7, 8 or 9 4 10, 11, or 12 5 13 or more 6	Windows in Front. State in this column the number of Windows in Front of House.	Tot the Figures you have entered in columns 6, 7, & 9, and enter the Total for each House in this column.
(Col. 1.)	(Col. 2.)	(Col. 3.)	(Col. 4.)	(Col. 5.)	(Col. 6.)	(Col. 7.)	(Col. 8.)	(Col. 9.)	(Col. 10.)
1	Built	Private Dwelling		Yes	1	1	3	1	6
2	"	"		Yes	1	1	3	1	6
3	"	"		Yes	1	1	3	3	8
4	"	"		Yes	1	1	3	3	8
5	"	"		Yes	1	1	3	3	8
6	"	"		Yes	1	1	3	3	8
7	"	"		Yes	1	1	2	3	7
8	"	"		Yes	1	1	3	3	8
9	"	"	1	Yes	1	1	2	4	8
9A	"	"		Yes	1	1	2	1	5
9B	"	Stable	1	No					
10	"	Private Dwelling		Yes	1	1	2	2	6
10A	"	"		Yes	1	1	2	1	5
11	"	"		Yes	1	1	2	2	6
11A	"	"		Yes	1	1	2	1	5
12	"	"		Yes	1	1	3	2	7
12A	"	"		Yes	1	1	2	1	5

Note B.—If one House is occupied by more than one Family, the Names of the Heads of Families so occupying it should be bracketed together

ELAND, 1911.

BUILDING RETURN.

Dublin **District Electoral Division,** _____ **Townland,** _____

Street, _S'Kevins Parade,_ **Parish,** _St Peters_

within and partly without a Parliamentary Borough, City, Urban District, Town, or Village, a *separate Return* should be made for each portion.

FAMILIES, &c.

No. of distinct Families in each House. (Col. 12.)	Name of the Head of each Family residing in the House. (Col. 13.)	No. of Rooms occupied by each Family. (See Note B at foot.) (Col. 14.)	Total Number of Persons in each Family. (Col. 15.)	Date on which Form A was collected. (Col. 14 f)	Number of Persons in each Family also who were sick on 2nd April 1911. (Col. 17.)	Name of the Landholder (if any) on whose Holding the House is situated, whether that name appears in column 13 or not. (Col. 18.)	No. on Form M.I. if House is on the Holding of a Landholder. (Col. 19.)
1	Patrick Bolger	6	6	1911 27th.4.11			
1	Ellias Lewis Rubinstein	6	8	"			
1	Yudel Myers	5	2	"			
1	Myre Rubinstein	5	11	"			
1	Abraham Goldberg	5	7	"			
1	Isaac Maslin	5	6	"			
1	Mathew Schrider	5	2	"			
1	Solomon Erulmonson	5	7	"			
1	David Isaacson	3½	4	"			
1	Nathan Levin	3	7	"			
1	Elizabeth Mulvey	4	5	"			
1	Sarah Sherley	3	5	"			
1	Joseph Flanagan	3	7	25th.4.0			
1	Thomas Irwin	3	3	"			
1	Solomon Gin	5	10	"			
1	Anna Browdy	3	2	"			

John Jones,
:— Peter Murray, } and the figure 1 entered in Col. 14, opposite the middle of the bracket. See pattern Table in Instructions, page 8. [OVER.

4590.11.11.11.5000 11,10,B.&N.,Ltd.—Ser. 90.

CENSUS O

Form N.—Enumerator's A

County *Borough of Dublin* Parliamentary Division} *St Patricks*   Poor Law Union} *South D*

Constabulary District *Dublin Metropolitan police*   City, Urban District, Tow

Sub-District ___*4 Division*___   Parliamentary Borough___

ABSTRACT showing the Number of Dwelling-houses, Families, and Persons in the above-named To
ascertained), of the People enumerated by *Michael McGeer o'C15e*

☞ Note.—This Abstract should be carefully filled by the Enumerator, and attached in front of the
the Townland or Street to which it relates.

When a Townland or Street is situated in two Parliamentary Divisions, or in more than one District Electoral Division or
Borough, City, Urban District, Town or Village, a separate Abstract should be made for each portion.

Approved,
J. B. DOUGHERTY,
Dublin Castle,
12th December, 1910.

WILLIAM J. THOMPSON,
Registrar-General,
EDWARD O'FARRELL,
DANIEL S. DOYLE,
} *Commissioners.*

No. on this Form	Number on Form B	DWELLING HOUSES. Inhabited	Un-inhabited	Building	FAMILIES. Number in each House	PERSONS. Males	Females	Total Number of Persons	Roman Catholics Males	Females	Protestant Episcop (See Note) Returning themselves as of "Church of Ireland" or "Irish Church" Males	Females	Males
1	1	1	-	-	1	4	2	6	4	2			
2	2	1	-	-	1	4	4	8	-	-			
3	3	1	-	-	1	1	1	2	-	-			
4	4	1	-	-	1	4	7	11	-	-			
5	5	1	-	-	1	3	4	7	-	-			
6	6	1	-	-	1	3	3	6	-	-			
7	7	1	-	-	1	1	1	2	-	-			
8	8	1	-	-	1	3	4	7	-	-			
9	9	1	-	-	1	2	2	4	-	-			
10	9A	1	-	-	1	3	4	7	-	-			
11	10	1	-	-	1	1	4	5	1	4	-	-	-
B². forled.,	1				11	29	36	65	5	6	-	-	-

NOTE.—The designation "Protestant Episcopalian" includes, besides the members of the "Church of Ireland" or "Iri

116

RELAND, 1911.

for a Townland or Street.

Dispensary
District *Electoral* { *South City N° 3*
Division

Dublin

Street, also the Religious Profession (so far as

several Forms for the persons enumerated in

partly within and partly without a Parliamentary

Townland } *St Stevens Parade*
or Street

Ward Barony *Wood Quay*

Parish *St Peters*

These Spaces will be filled up at the Gen...

74 *Wood Quay Ward (part of) in 91 files File 81*

RELIGIOUS PROFESSION.																No. on this Form
Presbyterians		Methodists		Independents		Baptists		Society of Friends or Quakers		Jews		All other Persuasions		Information refused		
Males	Females	Males	Females	Males	Females	Males	Females	Males	Fem.	Males	Fem.	Males	Fem.	Males	Fem.	
															•	1
										4	4					2
										1	1					3
										4	7					4
										3	4					5
										3	3					6
										1	1					7
										3	4					8
										2	2					9
	1									3	3					10
																11
	1									24	29					

be members of the Church of England, the Episcopal Church of Scotland, and any other Protestant Episcopal Church.

CENSUS O

Form N.—Enumerator's A

County _____

Parliamentary Division } *St Patricks*

Poor Law Union } *South D*

District District *A Division*

City, Urban District, Town

Sub-District _____

Parliamentary Borough

ABSTRACT showing the Number of Dwelling-houses, Families, and Persons in the above-named Tow ascertained), of the People enumerated by *Thomas Mc Nally P.C.109 A*

☞ Note.—This Abstract should be carefully filled by the Enumerator, and attached in front of the the Townland or Street to which it relates.

When a Townland or Street is situated in two Parliamentary Divisions, or in more than one District Electoral Division or Borough, City, Urban District, Town or Village, a separate Abstract should be made for each portion.

Approved,
D. HARREL,
Dublin Castle,
21st December, 1900.

ROBERT E. MATHESON,
Registrar-General,
T. J. BELLINGHAM BRADY,
ROBERT J. BREW,
} Commissione

No on this Form	Number on Form B	DWELLING HOUSES.			FAMILIES.	PERSONS.			Roman Catholics		Protestant Episcopal (See Note)		
		Inhabited	Un-inhabited	Building	Number in each House	Males	Females	Total Number of Persons			Returning themselves as of "Church of Ireland" or "Irish Church"		
									Males	Females	Males	Females	Males
1	1	1	—	—	1	4	2	6	4	2	—	—	—
2	2	1	—	—	1	1	1	2	—	—	—	—	—
3	3	1	—	—	1	2	3	5	—	—	—	—	—
4	4	1	—	—	1	2	1	3	—	—	—	—	—
5	5	1	—	—	1	5	2	7	—	1	—	—	—
6	6	1	—	—	1	4	2	6	—	1	—	—	—
7	7	1	—	—	1	2	3	5	—	—	—	—	—
8	8	1	—	—	1	5	5	10	—	—	—	—	—
9	9	1	—	—	1	2	3	5	—	—	—	—	—
10	10	1	—	—	1	1	4	5	1	4	—	—	—
11	11	1	—	—	1	2	3	5	2	3	—	—	—
B. forwd.,		11	—	—	11	30	29	59	7	11			

NOTE.—The designation "Protestant Episcopalian" includes, besides the members of the "Church of Ireland" or "Iri

IRELAND, 1901.

for a Townland or Street.

District Electoral Division

ge *Dublin*

Townland or Street *St Kevins Parade*

West Wood Quay

Parish *St Patricks*

Street, also the Religious Profession (so far as

several Forms for the persons enumerated in

is partly within and partly without a Parliamentary

These Spaces will be filled up at the Census Office

76

Dublin 79 fil... File 21

RELIGIOUS PROFESSION.

Presbyterians		Methodists		Independents		Baptists		Society of Friends or Quakers		Jews		All other Persuasions		Information refused		
Males	Females	Males	Females	Males	Females	Males	Females	Males	Fem.	Males	Fem.	Males	Fem.	Males	Fem.	
–	–	–	–	–	–	–	–	–	–	–	–	–	–	–	–	1
–	–	–	–	–	–	–	–	–	–	1	1	–	–	–	–	2
–	–	–	–	–	–	–	–	–	–	2	3	–	–	–	–	3
–	–	–	–	–	–	–	–	–	–	2	1	–	–	–	–	4
–	–	–	–	–	–	–	–	–	–	5	1	–	–	–	–	5
–	–	–	–	–	–	–	–	–	–	4	1	–	–	–	–	6
–	–	–	–	–	–	–	–	–	–	2	3	–	–	–	–	7
–	–	–	–	–	–	–	–	–	–	5	5	–	–	–	–	8
–	–	–	–	–	–	–	–	–	–	2	3	–	–	–	–	9
–	–	–	–	–	–	–	–	–	–	–	–	–	–	–	–	10
–	–	–	–	–	–	–	–	–	–	–	–	–	–	–	–	11
–	–	–	–	–	–	–	–	–	–	23	18	–	–	–	–	

the members of the Church of England, the Episcopal Church of Scotland, and any other Protestant Episcopal Church.

No. of Reference Map	Local Numbers	Streets, &c., and Occupiers	Immediate Lessors	Description of Tenement	Area A. R. P.	Land £ s. d.	Buildings £ s. d.	Total Annual Valuation of Rateable Property £ s.
		CLANBRASSIL-ST., UPPER—*continued.*						
5	5	Samuel Parker,	Elizabeth Nightingale,	House and small yard,	—	—	8 0 0	8 0
8	8	Thomas Harte and George Kellett,	Thomas Warren,	House and small yard,	—	—	19 0 0	19 0
9	1	—— Daly,	Thomas John Ousley,	House, yard, & sm. gar.	—	—	25 0 0	25 0
10	2	Rev. Wm. M. Mason,	Same,	House, yard, & sm. gar.	—	—	20 0 0	20 0
11	3	Thomas Phepoe,	Same,	House, yard, & sm. gar.	—	—	20 0 0	20 0
12	4	Agnes Byrne,	Same,	House, yard, & sm. gar.	—	—	21 0 0	21 0
13	5	Richard Cashell,	Same,	House, yard, & sm. gar.	—	—	21 0 0	21 0
1		Edm. Lawless (*lodgers*),	Edmond Lawless,	House,	—	—	8 0 0	8 0
2		Edm. Lawless (*lodgers*),	Same,	House,	—	—	8 0 0	8 0
3		Edm. Lawless (*lodgers*),	Same,	House,	—	—	8 0 0	8 0
4		Edm. Lawless (*lodgers*),	Same,	House,	—	—	8 0 0	8 0
5		Edm. Lawless (*lodgers*),	Same,	House,	—	—	8 0 0	8 0
6		Edm. Lawless (*lodgers*),	Same,	House,	—	—	8 0 0	8 0
28	18	Thomas Alwell,	Same,	House and rooms over gateway,	—	—	19 0 0	19 0
29	19	James Murphy,	Same,	House & small garden,	—	—	20 0 0	20 0
		COOK-STREET. (Ord. S. 20.)						
30	30	David Simpson (*lodgers*)	David Simpson,	House, rooms over gateway, and yard,	—	—	7 0 0	7 0
31	31	David Simpson (*lodgers*)	Same,	House and small yard,	—	—	8 0 0	8 0
35	35	John F. Nugent,	Monica Purcell,	House, workshop, yard, and small garden,	—	—	18 0 0	18 0
58	58	David Simpson,	Charles Kernan,	House and small yard,	—	—	10 0 0	10 0
59	59	David Simpson (*lodgers*),	David Simpson,	House and small yard,	—	—	9 0 0	9 0
		COOMBE. (Ord. S. 26.)						
87	87	Christr. Doyle (*lodgers*),	Christopher Doyle,	House,	—	—	6 0 0	6 0
38	38	Christr. Doyle (*lodgers*),	Same,	House, off., and sm. yard,	—	—	7 0 0	7 0
40	40	James Banahan (*lodgers*),	James Banahan,	House and yard,	—	—	6 0 0	6 0
41	41	James Banahan,	Thomas Sibthorpe,	House, office, and yard,	—	—	9 0 0	9 0
87	87	Vacant,	James Banahan,	Ho., bakery (*dilapd.*), &yd.	—	—	10 0 0	10 0
88	88	Vacant,	Same,	House and yard,	—	—	6 0 0	6 0
		CORK-STREET. (Ord. S. 25.)						
52	52	Joseph Butler,	Edward Atkinson,	Ho., offs, garden, & land,	4 0 32	15 0 0	40 0 0	55 0
		CORN-MARKET. (Ord. S. 20.)						
4	4	J. Dwyer (*lodgers*),	J. Dwyer,	Bakers' hall & rooms over	—	—	16 0 0	16 0
1		J. Dwyer (*lodgers*),	Same,	House,	—	—	12 0 0	12 0
2		J. Dwyer (*lodgers*),	Same,	House,	—	—	6 0 0	6 0
5	5	J. Dwyer (*lodgers*),	Same,	House and yard,	—	—	14 0 0	14 0
19	19	—— Hawkins,	Michael O'Neill,	House and small yard,	—	—	36 0 0	36 0
		CROSS-STICK-ALLEY. (Ord. S. 20.)						
5	4	Andrew M'Guirk,	Christopher Doyle,	House,	—	—	2 10 0	2 10
6	5	Thos. Sharkey (*lodgers*),	Thomas Sharkey,	House and yard,	—	—	2 10 0	2 10
		DEAN-STREET. (Ord. S. 20.)						
7	7	Charles Ryan,	Richard Walsh & others,	House, office, and yard,	—	—	50 0 0	50 0

4 *Example of a primary (or Griffith's) valuation, 1854*

However, the compilers' notebooks containing this information still survive in the Royal Irish Academy in Dublin, and deal with 19 of the 32 Irish counties.

Those from Antrim and Derry contain lists of emigrants, the names of which have been extracted, arranged alphabetically under parish, and published as *Irish Emigration Lists 1833–1839: Lists of Emigrants Extracted from the Ordnance Survey Memoirs for Counties Londonderry and Antrim*, under the direction of Brian Mitchell, by the Genealogical Publishing Co. Inc., Baltimore 1989.

These emigration lists differ from American customs passenger lists in that they show both the place of origin in Ireland, and the destination in America, together with the age, townland address, year of departure, and religion, for the 3,000 plus emigrants mentioned in the book. Unfortunately, such emigration lists were not compiled for any of the other counties.

Return of owners of land in Ireland

In 1873 the Local Government Board launched a type of modern Domesday survey to find out the numbers and names of all owners of land of one acre and more. Similar schemes were also carried out in England and Wales. Poor Law Unions were required to supply information on landowners, from their own valuations and rate books, and the subsequent returns were made to the Local Government Board. The details were arranged under county, put into alphabetical order, and published in a Government Paper in 1876 as 'A Return of Owners of Land of One Acre and Upwards in the Several Counties, Counties of Cities, and Counties of Towns in Ireland.'

The named land owners so listed amounted to 32,614, the unnamed ones (owning less than one acre) numbering 36,114. Returns should be initially researched province by province, then by county, and finally by surname. The address, acreage owned, and valuation of the property should then be found.

Tithe composition applotment books

According to the Tithe Composition Act of 1823, provision was made for Church of Ireland clergy to receive any tithes due to them in money instead of in kind. The Act generated a series of surveys carried out between 1823 and 1837, in order to establish just what was owed, where, and by whom.

The books were compiled under parishes, but only in rural areas, not in towns and cities, where 'kind' was not likely to be forthcoming in any case. Tithes due were levied on agricultural holdings kept by Catholics and Protestants alike, regardless of whether or not they were members of the Church of Ireland, so the result of these surveys is a list of land-tenants of all denominations. Books were produced for each rural parish, giving the names of the occupiers, the amount of land held and the sum due. If one bears in mind that a tithe represents one-tenth of a person's wealth, the relative status of an individual may be roughly estimated from his contributions.

Thousands of returns, written in manuscript, are now in the Public Record Office, with a volume for each county of the Republic, showing the parishes in which surnames listed are to be found. Returns for the Six Counties are kept in Belfast in the PRO of Northern Ireland. Surname indexes for all thirty-two counties, on both sides of the Border, are available in major Irish libraries.

Hearth money rolls

Also known as 'Smoke Silver', hearth money was levied by an Act of Parliament in 1663, and was similar to the English Hearth Tax in that it imposed a tax (in this case 2s) on every hearth and fireplace. Initially payable at Lady Day and Michaelmas, it later became payable on the 10th of January each year, and was collected by the Sheriff of each county and his henchmen.

The system of collection was open to abuse by those administering it in that the less scrupulous among them left, not only with the tax itself, but also with what little household goods the peasants owned.

The hearth-owners are listed alphabetically under county, barony, parish, and finally townland, and collections were arranged over large areas known as 'walks'; the number of hearths and the amount of tax payable also appear. The poor are included in the earlier rolls, but were later exempt; thus the first one represents a list of virtually all householders, with some indication of their social and economic standing. However, as with any listing, one has no means of telling the ages and relationships of persons mentioned in them, and they are therefore much inferior

TOWNLAND	NAMES OF OCCUPIERS	Plantation TITHEABLE Measure												
		Quantities in Detail			Quality	Total Quantity in Holding			Total Quantity in Townland			Annual Value of Holding			Real Acreable Value
		A	R	P		A	R	P	A	R	P	£	s	d	£	s	d
					Smughtsonweir	71	0	0				277	14	0½			
	Drew Nicholas	5	1	5	Arable Meadow & Pasture	5	1	5				21	2	6	4	0	0
		0	0	14	Garden	0	0	14				0	7	0	4	0	0
	Corbelly Elias	0	0	17	D°	0	0	17				0	8	6	4	0	0
	Cunningham Hugh	0	0	23	D°	0	0	23				0	11	6	4	0	0
	Mangan Edw.	5	2	0	Arable Meadow & Pasture	5	2	0				22	0	0	4	0	0
		3	0	9	D°	3	0	9				12	4	6	4	0	0
	Wise Elias	0	0	3	Garden	0	0	3				0	1	6	4	0	0
	Cox Walter	2	3	0	Arable Meadow & Pasture	2	3	0				11	0	0	4	0	0
	Gorman Widow	3	2	30	D°	3	2	30				14	15	0	4	0	0
	Dannelly Mary	1	1	33	D°	1	1	33				5	1	11½	3	10	0
	Shaw John	0	1	7	Garden	0	1	7				1	3	0	4	0	0
Finglass East	Mc Guire	0	0	1	D°	0	0	1				0	0	0	4	0	0
		0	0	6	D°	0	0	6				0	3	0	4	0	0
	Reddy Benj.	2	2	12	Arable Meadow & Pasture	2	2	12				10	6	0	4	0	0
		16	2	10	D°										4	0	0
		19	2	36	D°										3	15	0
		36	1	14		36	1	14				140	8	4½			
	Shaw Jane	37	2	27	D°	37	2	27				150	13	6	4	0	0
		2	1	8	D°	2	1	8				9	4	0	4	0	0
		0	2	13	Garden	0	2	13				2	6	6	4	0	0
		0	0	11	D°	0	0	11				0	5	6	4	0	0
	Henshall Mess	1	3	34	Arable Meadow & Pasture	1	3	34				7	17	0	4	0	0
		0	3	7	D°	0	3	7				3	3	6	4	0	0
	Smyth Patk. H.	0	1	24	D°	0	1	24				1	12	0	4	0	0
		0	1	0	Garden	0	1	0				1	0	0	4	0	0
						176	1	18				693	9	10			

5 *Tithe composition applotment book entry. 1833*

to parish records or civil registration certificates in their value to family historians.

Poll tax

In 1660 a poll tax was introduced, whereby anyone aged twelve years or over was liable to pay tax, and the returns thus obtained give some details of individuals.

Miscellaneous records

Any area will produce its own outstanding families, estates, buildings, and indeed events, which will generate records. Unfortunately the lack of county record offices, with their vast stores of local documents, manuscripts, printed matter, and staff who are especially knowledgeable about their districts, as in England and Wales, means that the researcher in Ireland will have a lengthy search ahead of him if he is to attempt to seek out all that may be in existence on the subject of his family or area, and it will normally entail a visit to Dublin or Belfast. The setting up of local Heritage Centres (see p. 169) will however, it is hoped, cut down considerably on the labour involved.

Parish registers

Roman Catholic registers
Because Irish Census returns are so scarce, Roman Catholic registers are more important sources for the family historian than their counterparts in Britain, particularly as regards the latter half of the nineteenth century when they become more numerous. Unfortunately, many registers do not start until the 1880s, counties with late-starting ones being most of those in Ulster (including Donegal), Galway and, in particular, Mayo.

The county having the earliest registers is Wexford (1671) but entries are often illegible, and the registers themselves are badly kept. The only other seventeenth-century entries are baptisms from St Nicholas's church, Galway, and these exist only for nine months in 1690. On the whole, registers for city parishes begin earlier than those for the more remote, rural ones, in contrast to the trend in Britain where new urban parishes appeared, and country ones were divided up, throughout the nineteenth century.

6 *Roman Catholic dioceses*

The majority of Irish Catholic registers start around the 1830s, and six of the twenty-six Catholic dioceses (those of Achonry, Clogher, Clonfert, Dromore, Killala and Raphoe) have no pre-1800 registers at all. Curiously, Catholic priests were never required by law to keep registers, so that some parishes never had them, while other registers were thrown away when full up, or when the families in them had died out or left the district.

There are several reasons for the inefficiency and lack of enthusiasm shown in the upkeep and care of registers. One of the principal ones is the fact that the Penal Laws made Catholics (not only in Ireland, but throughout the British Isles) very wary about allowing any information to be written down if it concerned religion, and thus could be used against them at some future date. Then, there was the lack of compulsion to keep records in the first place; and, lastly, the battering which the books themselves suffered while being carried around the parish to chapels of ease spread out over a large area, or backwards and forwards to marriages in private houses. To save carrying the actual register with them on these jaunts, some priests would often jot down notes about the ceremony on scraps of paper: these, human nature being what it is, were only too frequently mislaid and not rediscovered until long after the event itself, to be then miscopied, guessed at, or even lost altogether.

Entries which did find their way intact into the register, and so down to us, may be written in either English or Latin depending on the inclination of the individual priest; luckily they were never kept in Irish! Latin is found more commonly than English in the earlier registers, and in the Irish-speaking Gaeltachtai where less people 'had the English'.

All post-1922 Irish Catholic registers are nowadays held in the parish. Of those already deposited prior to 1922 in the PRO, 817 were destroyed, although some had been transcribed previously. A list of survivors is kept in the Reading Room of the PRO.

In the 1960s, however, the National Library of Ireland microfilmed more than 90% of Catholic registers, from their beginnings until about 1880. Those which were *not* filmed are those from Dublin City, three parishes in the diocese of Ardagh and Clonmacnoise, and some others from Leitrim.

It is no longer necessary to obtain written permission from the parish priest before one may consult the microfilms, as once was the case, apart from those films containing registers from the dioceses of Ardagh and Clonmacnoise, Cloyne, Down and Connor, Galway, Kerry, and Limerick.

The Irish government has recently financed a series of schemes designed to index records of historical interest, including, of course, parish registers. It is anticipated that a centre will eventually be set up for each county in the Republic, and that the indexes of all findings will be put on computer.

From these schemes has developed the Irish Family History Society, which may be contacted at William Street, Tullamore, Co. Offaly, for information on current projects and their locations; another contact is the Family History Council of Ireland (which includes the Six Counties).

Catholic parish registers for the nine Ulster counties (the Six, plus Cavan, Donegal, and Monaghan) are on microfilm at the PRONI, in Belfast.

The Church of Ireland

Registers were not obligatory in the Church of Ireland until 1634, nearly a full century after Thomas Cromwell's Injunction concerning England and Wales in 1538. Some parishes in Ireland, though, must have already started keeping them before this was made compulsory, as the oldest C of I registers extant are believed to be those of St John's church, Dublin, which begin in 1619. The only Anglican dioceses not to have records from at least 1750 onwards are Achonry, Emly, Kilfenora, Kilmacduagh and Killala, where Protestants were very much in the minority, even by Irish standards.

On the whole, the standard of record-keeping is not high, the writing being frequently bad, as is the spelling, even when one takes into account the lack of concern about 'correct' spelling at this period.

7 *Church of Ireland dioceses*

The majority of C of I registers remain in the parish, although some pre-1870 ones are in the PRO, and are listed in the Reading Room there.

Acts of 1875 and 1876 decreed that all pre-Disestablishment registers (that is prior to 1869) should become public records. Of the 1600-plus Anglican parishes, about two thirds deposited their registers in the PRO in the Four Courts. There had been a suggestion made that they should be housed in the General Register Office but tragically, although this was a popular idea, it was not adopted.

On 30 June 1922, during the Civil War, the Four Courts exploded into flames and the PRO was burnt to the ground. Most of its priceless manuscripts were lost; some were blown away and recovered as far as ten miles off.

Of the 1,006 Anglican registers deposited, only four survived, the worst losses to family historians being the registers from small rural parishes, covering a long timespan; however, these only contained a small number of entries.

Fortunately, many transcripts and abstracts had already been made, and occasionally these still come to light in unexpected places; they are kept in the PRO with microfilm copies of the survivors. In addition to keeping the actual parish registers themselves, Church of Ireland incumbents used to compile Parochial Returns, or extracts from their registers (which are similar to English Bishops' Transcripts) some of which survive also.

Church of Ireland registers may be found in various places; they are not necessarily kept in the parish when completed as are Roman Catholic ones, neither are they all in the PRO. It is therefore essential to find out whether originals or copies of a certain register exist, and whereabouts they are held.

The Representative Church Body Library (RCBL) at Braemor Park, Dublin 14, holds many originals, the numbers increasing annually as more parish churches close.

The most likely place to find at least a reference to the register needed is the PRO which keeps two lists of all known registers, with the exception of those from Dublin City.

The first list, known as the Church of Ireland Parish Register Index, was compiled from inventories drawn up after the Acts of 1875 and 1876 converting all pre-Disestablishment registers into public records. Despite subsequent corrections, it is, of course, out of date. Copies of this list can be found in the National Library and the Genealogical Office, but these are more in need of updating than that in the PRO.

The second list, that of Parish Registers and Related Material, as it is called, has been recently compiled from both manuscript and typed lists of PRO holdings. It consists of the four surviving original registers, three sets of Parochial Returns, assorted copies of registers, and the searches made by the PRO when looking for the dates of birth of those applying for state pensions when they were introduced in 1909; these baptisms will date from the 1830s and 1840s.

If the PRO can offer no solutions, then the PRO of Northern Ireland should be approached if the register is one from an Ulster parish; failing this, the RCBL, as mentioned above.

Lastly, it is worth contacting the incumbent of the parish itself; his name and address will be listed in the current *Church of Ireland Directory*.

As regards the City of Dublin, its parishes have had a good number of copies and abstracts made (for a list compiled by E. J. McAuliffe, see *The Irish Genealogist*, Vol. 5, pages 267–9). Dublin records are housed in the PRO, the RCBL, the National Library, Trinity College Manuscript Library, and in the actual parishes. The Parish Record Society of Dublin has published contents of more than twenty registers, mostly from the city, from work carried out in the early part of this century.

In Belfast, the PRONI has microfilms of all surviving registers from the nine Ulster counties. Microfilming is organized at diocesan level, not recognizing political boundaries, and so certain parishes from Cos. Leitrim and Louth are also included where forming part of an Ulster diocese. PRONI films of the registers of St Anne's Cathedral, Belfast, St John's, Malone, Belfast, and Lisburn Cathedral, plus lists of parishes in the Republic filmed by the Belfast Office, are to be found in the RCBL.

During the period 1959–63 the PRONI microfilmed pre-Disestablishment records from those which survived from the Republic. Most parishes in sixteen dioceses in Connacht and Munster were included, namely: Achonry, Ardfert and Aghadoe, Cashel, Clonfert, Cloyne, Cork, Emly, Kilfenora, Killala, Killaloe, Kilmacduagh, Limerick, Lismore, Ross, Tuam and Waterford.

A second stage, begun in 1975, included all survivors from the dioceses of Meath, Kildare, Glendalough and, later, Ferns. Also filmed were vestry-books (records of early Parochial Church Council meetings) and post-Disestablishment records. The latter are not classified as public records, and so access is not permitted to them without express permission from the clergyman of the parish concerned.

Perhaps it should be mentioned that these survivors are registers which were not deposited in the PRO in the first place, rather than those four which survived the destruction of the Office.

The earliest C of I register listed in the PRO is that of Drumglass, Co. Tyrone, which is said to date from 1600; but the newer PRONI index shows that the baptismal entries date from only 1665, so it is dangerous to take listings and indexes at their face value without consulting the actual registers, if this is at all possible.

Unfortunately it is difficult to search C of I registers, even in transcript, without going to Ireland yourself, or finding a contact who is willing to undertake work on your behalf. Some printed transcripts and pedigrees appear in *The Irish Genealogist*, and the Society of Genealogists' Library contains transcripts of three registers and a marriage index for the Limerick diocese, compiled by Brian de Breffny, but apart from these, copies of registers are very thin on the ground outside Ireland itself.

Presbyterian records
In view of the Presbyterian Church's chequered history, it is hardly surprising that its records are in a somewhat chaotic state. In the eighteenth century, all non-Anglicans, not just Catholics, were subject to the Penal Laws. Until 1782, marriages performed by clergymen who were not members of the Church of Ireland were considered illegal, with the exception of Catholics married by Catholic priests.

Many people thus discriminated against emigrated to America in search of freedom of worship, thus starting a precedent: no less than five American presidents, Jackson, Polk, Buchanan, Arthur and McKinley, were of Presbyterian-Irish stock. Membership of the Church today is usually a sign of earlier Scottish ancestry, the denomination having its roots in that country.

Some Presbyterian baptism and marriage records go back to the seventeenth century, and most of these older registers are lodged with The Presbyterian Historical Society, Room 218, 2nd Floor,

Church House, Fisherwick Place, Belfast BT1 6DW, where they form the only centralized collection.

The Historical Society also keeps copies of the 1766 Religious Census for much of Ulster; lists of Protestant householders compiled in 1775, for Antrim, Derry and Donegal; Presbyterian Census Returns – unique to the Church – for 1775; and Certificates of Transference, which were character references issued to persons who left the parish to live in another. The Society's premises are open Monday, Tuesday, Thursday and Friday, from 10 am to 12.30 pm, and on Wednesday from 10 am to 1 pm, and from 2 pm to 4 pm.

Other registers are held by the Church ministers, and the majority of them date from the 1830s and 1840s. In 1819 a synod decided to record baptisms and marriages, but many churches must have already started to do so by then. As Presbyterian marriages were not legal for the period 1839 to 1844, though, along with all other Non-Conformist marriages, and there are no Presbyterian burial entries, the Church of Ireland registers must be searched for these events.

No accurate listing of baptism and marriage registers exists, the next best thing for most people being Margaret Falley's book, *Irish and Scotch-Irish Ancestral Research*. This lists registers of more than 350 congregations and is particularly strong in its bibliographical section. It first appeared in 1962, and was reprinted by the Genealogical Publishing Co. in 1988.

A very welcome addition to Irish family history bookshelves is *A Guide to Irish Parish Registers* by Brian Mitchell, from the same publishers, 1988, which provides listings of existing Irish registers, of all denominations, together with their starting dates and locations. Moreover, it offers help in using parish registers in conjunction with the Griffith's Valuation 1848–1864, as complementary tools for the historian's use when attempting to reconstruct life in a Victorian civil parish.

At the PRO of Northern Ireland is a typed index of the Six Counties, compiled by parish, and giving details of those registers which are available; this is being revised to cover all nine Ulster counties. Copies of this index are held by the PRONI itself, the Presbyterian Historical Society, and the local congregation. The PRONI is in the process of copying all Ulster records, some in typescript form, the most recent on microfilm.

The Presbyterian Historical Society is working on a new index to its manuscript records, arranged alphabetically, under congregations. The Society holds valuable transcripts of petitions of Dissenters presented to the Irish Parliament in 1775, as already mentioned, the originals having been destroyed in 1922; these cover Antrim, Armagh, Derry, Down, Tyrone and Dublin.

The majority of Irish Presbyterians today live in Ulster, although they are to be found all over Ireland. Due to the fact that Presbyterianism is on the decline in the Republic, churches close, and their registers are sent either to the church with which they are to be amalgamated, or to the Historical Society in Belfast.

Presbyterians are not easy to trace as they have no rigid parish organization, members being free to attend the church of their choice. In addition many churches had only a short lifespan, so identifying them can prove difficult, as can listing them. For churches known to be in use today, and part of the General Assembly (there are two other bodies, the Reformed Presbyterian Church, and the Non-Subscribers) consult the *Presbyterian Church in Ireland Directory*, which appears annually and is obtainable in libraries, or from the Historical Society.

Other Non-Conformist denominations

Early nineteenth-century Irish *Methodists* enjoyed very close links with their Anglican neighbours, and the two sets of clergymen appear to have baptized the offspring of each other's congregations indiscriminately.

Few Methodist registers exist from before 1820, the earliest being from 1816; registers remain with the church ministers. Marriage entries start about 1845, on average, while burial registers do not exist, deceased Methodists, like other non-Anglicans, being interred by the local C of I clergyman, and the event recorded in his parish register.

Registers of the *Society of Friends*, or Quakers, date from the mid-seventeenth century, and record baptisms, marriages and deaths (not burials). Quaker marriage certificates are enormous, including the signatures of all the wedding guests!

Quaker records for Munster, Connaught and Leinster (except for those for Cavan, which are missing) are kept at the Friends' Meeting House, Eustace Street, Dublin, where personal visits may be arranged on Thursday mornings. Apart from recorded baptisms, marriages and deaths, the Dublin Meeting House can offer a wide range of sources: six manuscript volumes of Quaker wills, the majority being seventeenth- and eighteenth-century; journals and diaries; details of relief work undertaken during the 1840s famine; minute books of Meetings, some of which give information about individual families; a file of manuscript pedigrees; Books of Disownment, which can be both amusing and informative.

In the Society's Historical Library are some 3,000 letters sent by, and to, Friends. The Library staff will undertake research for a reasonable fee. In Ulster, the Friends' Meeting House, at Lisburn, Co. Antrim, keeps records of Quakers, both in Ulster and beyond the province. A useful publication, *A Guide to Irish Quaker Records*, by Olive C. Goodbody, is on sale at the Government Publications Sales Office, GPO Arcade, Dublin.

When undertaking research among early Quaker records, it must be remembered that, until 1754, the Society used the Old Style calendar whereby the year began on Lady Day (25th March) instead of 1st January as today. Elsewhere the New Style calendar came into effect in September 1752. Quakers would also refer to the months of the year by numbers, instead of by name.

The conscientious and often highly-skilled French Protestants known as *Huguenots*, who left their own country to escape religious persecution, have several cemeteries in Dublin.

Literature concerning Huguenots is available at Marsh's Library, St Patrick's Close, Dublin. It may also be worthwhile contacting: The Huguenot Society of London, c/o Barclays Bank plc., Pall Mall, London, for general information on Huguenot ancestors.

The *Palatines* were refugees from the Rhineland Palatinate who, at the beginning of the eighteenth century, were driven from their homeland by the combined effects of French invasion and starvation brought about by severe winter weather.

Initially they were supposed to go to Pennsylvania, to settle on land given them by the government, but many ended up in England instead. Their numbers soon made them unpopular, and they were sent off from London to destinations such as Sunderland, Ireland and even Jamaica. By August 1709 the first 794 families were packed off to Ireland, with others following; within a year, a total of 3,073 Palatines had arrived.

The Crown set aside £15,000, paid over three years, for their maintenance; this quickly attracted the interest of landlords in

Ireland but, by November 1711, about 232 families had already had enough of Ireland and returned to London. Others followed, all complaining of hostile treatment at the hands of their Catholic neighbours who, naturally enough, resented these privileged Protestant foreigners in their midst.

Many Palatines, though, stayed on to work in Dublin, and others were sent to Co. Limerick, where they established settlements of their own. In 1745 they were visited by no less a personage than John Wesley, who expressed disgust at their drunkenness and profanity, but noted that they had no decent Protestant clergy to care for their spiritual wellbeing. Wesley had a sharp word with the powers-that-be and on his return in 1760 found things much improved; many Palatines then became Methodists. Two of them who emigrated from Limerick that year, Philip Embury and Barbara Heck, founded the Methodist Church in North America. About this time Palatine fortunes declined and many left Ireland, although new settlements were formed in the mid-west of the country.

By the early nineteenth century they had ceased to speak German, and had largely intermarried with local families, usually Protestant ones. They had built up an enviable reputation for hard work and upright living and, during the famine, were a source of great help and comfort to their Catholic neighbours.

By the early twentieth century some Palatine surnames were still recognizable as such, although many were, and are, identical to British ones, like Baker, and Smith, Miller and Long. This is generally due to the changes of name which many of them assumed, sometimes more than once, in order to fit in with the host community.

When dealing with Palatine ancestors, then, one has the usual problems of entries being lost in the fire of 1922 and, in addition, that of name changes over the years. Further elucidation is provided in a useful article by J. L. Alton, which appeared in *Family Tree Magazine*, vol. 3, No. 4, February 1987 (from which the above information is gratefully taken); for a study in depth, Alton in turn recommends *The Early-eighteenth-century Palatine Emigration*, by W. A. Knittle, University of Pennsylvania doctoral thesis, 1936.

INTERPRETING THE RECORDS: BIRTHS, MARRIAGES AND DEATHS

Irish birth certificates

The information contained on Irish birth certificates differs slightly from that on British ones as it consists of: place of birth; parents' names; the mother's maiden name; date of birth; residence and occupation of the father.

They are not always reliable as there were plenty of faults and omissions. What would seem to be a curiously Irish weakness is that, by the time the parents got round to registering the fact, the actual date of birth had sometimes been forgotten! On other occasions, the baptismal entry has been found to precede the registered date of birth, as wrongly 'remembered' by the informant. Some eager parents registered their offspring's birth before they had chosen a Christian name and so the infant appears merely as 'M' or 'F'; this sometimes happened with English birth registrations as well.

Births suspected to have taken place at sea should be looked for in the General Registrar's Office in Dublin, where they will be found as certified by British consuls abroad 1864–1921.

Catholic baptisms

As with any country, it is necessary to remember that the date of baptism is not necessarily immediately after that of birth, although christenings normally took place within a matter of weeks, particularly in Catholic families who believed that an unbaptized child was consigned to limbo instead of going straight to heaven.

Although Irish Catholic registers are recent compared with many British ones, only about one tenth of parishes having baptismal registers dating from the eighteenth century, they are helpful in that they give the names of the child's sponsors or godparents, who were usually relatives. This gives the researcher a chance to cast his net a little further afield and find details of related and intermarried families. Another useful bonus is the inclusion of the mother's maiden name and, with luck, the parents' townland and even, occasionally, the actual address.

Unfortunately, it is rare to find mention of the father's occupation, as occurs in other British registers from at least the mid-nineteenth century onwards. How much simpler it would be for us if the Irish had used the Welsh system of distinguishing between individuals of the same surname and we could tell Murphy the Milk from Murphy the Meat.

Adding to the confusion is the persistent Irish habit of naming the eldest son after the husband's paternal grandfather and the second son for the maternal one. Similarly, the two oldest daughters would be called after their respective great-grandmothers. This pattern becomes plain when enough generations of the family are committed to paper but, until the individuals concerned have been correctly identified, it certainly does not make research any easier.

Church of Ireland baptisms

The baptismal entries in Anglican registers are in almost direct contrast with their Catholic counterparts in that few godparents are listed and it is unusual to find any mention of the mother's maiden name, except in Ulster, where the Scottish practice of doing so is followed. As in earlier English registers, the mother is sometimes not referred to at all, as if the infant was nothing whatsoever to do with her!

There is often compensation, though, with the inclusion of the father's address and occupation. Most C of I registers will contain a considerable number of Methodist baptisms and vice-versa; see the section of 'Other Non-Conformist denominations' earlier in this chapter (p. 132).

Illegitimacy

In medieval Celtic society a child born out of wedlock could have its father 'named' by the mother. The person thus chosen was usually a leading figure in the community and he would usually agree to accept the role. In actual fact, he could well have been the natural father, as such men bestowed their favours around the females of the district in true seigniorial fashion. Under the old Celtic, or Brehon, law no inequality existed between legitimate and illegitimate children, the bloodline being seen as of more importance.

This casual attitude towards bastardy, not surprisingly, was thoroughly disapproved of by the English who viewed such laxity as a threat to their own system of inheritance and a habit that was probably catching! One imagines too that there would have been a certain element of jealousy involved, and the English hastened to 'improve' Irish morals in much the same way that their descendants were to chastise the native Africans for their nakedness and supposed immorality.

An opposite view of the Irish in later centuries was advanced in an article written by K. H. Connell, in 1950, for the *Economic History Review*. Entitled 'Land and population in Ireland 1780–1845', it quotes contemporary writers, many of them English and with no particular love for the Irish, who nevertheless stated that illegitimacy was rare in rural Ireland. A certain Col. Colby, in charge of the Ordnance Survey in the 1830s, went so far as to say that, because of the purity of Irish girls, some 800 of his English workers had taken Irish wives.

One reason for all this chastity was almost certainly the influence of the clergy in discouraging incontinence in the first place or, failing this, to bring about wedlock before the prospective bastard put in an appearance. High marriage rates and early marriages at this period would seem to have been an even greater factor in removing the opportunity in the first place.

Where girls did produce illegitimate children, the fact is always noted against baptismal entries. Ways of expressing such a calamity vary from the mild observation 'natural child', or 'out of wedlock', through to the brutal 'bastard' written with venom across the entry itself.

Marriage in Ireland

In the middle ages the native Irish favoured civil rather than church weddings. Even as late as the sixteenth century the Attorney General for Ireland, an Englishman named Sir John Popham, claimed that only about one in twenty Irish marriages took place in church, probably because the bride's house was, and remained, a popular venue. The ceremony was, of course, still performed by a priest.

Other marriages varied from casual, although not necessarily promiscuous, relationships to serious partnerships; while both polygamy and polyandry seem to have been perfectly acceptable practices, depending on the current marital needs of the individual community.

Women must have enjoyed a better status under the Brehon law than their descendants did either under the Church of Rome or the English Crown. Even up to our own time marriage in Ireland, far from being made in heaven, was a matter of cash, land and property. Combined with the material assets which a potential bride might be expected to offer, her qualities as breeding-stock had to be assessed, not to mention her talents as a farm worker.

The following article, here slightly abridged, was written by Mrs Ann Hamerton for the Oxford University Staff Association Journal and describes her own observations of rural Irish life, just over the Border into Ulster. She is talking about a war-blinded ex-serviceman and his attempts to settle down into civilian life once more.

> Most of the men who, like him, had some peripheral vision, could manage a small farm quite well, with the help of a competent wife. Alfie was not so blessed. His wife was what is known in Ireland as a Poor Creature, mildly consumptive and suffering from fits, but nevertheless producing a new baby each year with unfailing regularity. Incited thereto by her doctor, my father [also a doctor] once ventured to suggest that, in view of her health, perhaps ten children were enough, but, with an unusual show of spirit, she retorted, 'My Alfie's a Poor Blind Man, and he must have *some* hobby'. When Alfie's hobby had resulted in thirteen children, she suffered a fit, fell into the fire and died of her burns.

Alfie then proceeded to solve the problem of who should look after the children, not to mention himself and the farm, by inviting Tilly, the local lady of easy virtue, to move in with him. Luckily all turned out well, for the farm prospered and all the children were 'happy, healthy and relatively clean'. When the subject of marriage was broached:

> Alfie mumbled something about the problems of both leaving the farm at once, the expense of bus fares into town to see the priest, pressure of work due to the potato harvest. 'A pity', my

father observed offhandedly, 'It'd make a big difference to your pension'. A short silence then, 'I never thought of that', said Alfie with great simplicity. The banns were read the following Sunday and, in due course, they were married, with an accompaniment of thirteen little bridesmaids and pages.

One morning a telegram arrived for my father which read: 'COME AT ONCE DAISY IS TOOK BAD ALFIE'. Problem: which of the thirteen children was Daisy? A telephone call to the local doctor established that all the children were well, but that Tilly was in bed with bronchitis. (Tilly – Daisy, it must be the Post Office again!) When he arrived he found Alfie bending solicitously over a swaddled figure tossing fretfully on the sofa, which was drawn up to the kitchen fire. 'Well, how are you, Tilly my dear?' he asked, leaning over the back of the sofa. A large pig stared up at him. This, it seemed, was Daisy, who had just produced seventeen piglets and was now 'took bad' with milk fever. Exactly what my father was supposed to do about it was not clear; he did, however, manage to do something about poor Tilly, wheezing away uncomplainingly in an unheated bedroom with not enough blankets because most of the family's supply had been needed for the ailing Daisy. After all, a good sow is a valuable animal.

Since the Famine the Irish seem to have been remarkably reluctant to marry. A phenomenon noticeable even today is their low rate of nuptiality, many couples being almost into middle age when they do get round to marrying; this is in direct contrast to earlier practice when, apart from those who went into monasteries and convents, most people married, and married young, a fact noted by William Cobbett in the 1770s.

All sorts of reasons have been put forward to explain this tardiness: lack of finances; unwillingness on the part of the man's father to relinquish any share in the family holding; the fact that, throughout history, Irish holdings have been too poor to support more than one family and that barely above subsistence level; the lack of opportunity to meet a suitable partner; and lastly, a conscious attempt at birth-control by reducing the number of years the woman would be fertile after marriage.

While any, or all, of these factors may be relevant, it is difficult to see why they should not apply to the European peasantry as a whole or, indeed, to the Irish themselves in earlier days. It has been pointed out by social historians, for example Peter Laslett in *The World We Have Lost Further Explored*, that the idea that our ancestors in England married very young is a fallacy; on the contrary, many of them actually had to postpone marrying until a suitable 'slot' in their community became vacant and, until that time, social approval of the proposed union was withheld.

Recent figures for the average age on marriage in Ireland continue the tradition of later marriage. In 1975, in the Republic, the average age for males was 27 years and for females 24.7 years, while in Northern Ireland in 1977 the respective ages were 25.3 for men and 23.2 for women.

The *Ulster Year Book 1986* gives figures for marriages by denomination, for 1981, which are as follows:

Roman Catholic	38.7%
Presbyterian	23.4%
C of I	16.3%
Other	9.6%
Civil	12.0%

These, when compared with the figures already shown for membership of each denomination, show that, in 1981 at least, the proportion of Catholics marrying in Ulster was comparatively high, but one must take into account the fact that civil marriages would account for a number of Protestant rather than Catholic weddings. Nevertheless, Catholic marriages, by percentage, remain above the rest.

Catholic marriages

According to an Act of 1746, which came into effect on 1st May of that year, any marriage solemnized by a Catholic priest was null and void if either of the partners was, or ever had been, Protestant. If both parties were Catholic, the marriage would be valid.

Under the first stage of Civil Registration in 1845, Catholic marriages were not required to be registered and indeed were not until full registration began in 1864. Catholic marriage registers contain the names of two witnesses who were usually related to the couple in some way, but unfortunately the names of the two sets of parents do not normally appear in early entries. The bride's address is often given and sometimes that of the groom. After 1860, more details are included: the names of all the parents, together with their addresses and those of the witnesses, which will probably give a clue to related families and their places of origin.

Rather surprisingly, it was not until the late nineteenth century that marriages began to take place in a church which was not the bride's parish one, there not being the wanderlust or amount of employment away from home which was a feature of the English working-classes by this period. Many weddings were still celebrated in the bride's home, as is legal today in Scotland and the United States, but not in England or Wales. The middle classes, however, tended to marry in Dublin, particularly if it were a second marriage for either party.

Church of Ireland marriages

Normally Irish Anglican marriage entries were neither signed nor witnessed, nor are the names of parents given prior to Civil Registration in 1864. These registers compare very unfavourably, then, with other British ones for the same period and indeed with Roman Catholic ones, for the researcher is deprived of the essential information concerning the couple's parentage (extra important if this is the woman's second marriage) and whether or not the parents were still alive at the time of the ceremony.

Marriage licence bonds

As in England, C of I marriages could be conducted after either the publishing of banns, or the purchase of a licence. Prior to about 1870, though, banns were looked down on as being somewhat vulgar and were called principally in the case of working-class weddings.

Before a licence could be issued, the bishop of the diocese in which the couple intended to marry required the groom and another surety (usually a relative of the bride) to enter into a bond to the effect that there was no 'just cause or impediment' to their forthcoming union.

This undertaking was seen as a safeguard for the bishop, as well as a deterrent to the bigamously inclined, and by the time that all the formalities had been taken care of, one presumes that most couples must have been certain that they really did want to go through with it. If the couple lived in different dioceses, the bond was normally taken out in that where the bride resided.

MARRIAGES solemnized in the Parish of _Inch & Killgorman_ in the County of _Wexford_ In the Year 18_32_

_3_

Hugh Butler, Knockenross of _the_ Parish _of Arklow_
and _Ellen McClean, Coolgreeny_ of _the_ Parish _Inch & Killgorman_
were married in this _Church_ by _Banns_ with Consent of _her Mother_ this _Twenty seventh_ Day of _November_ in the Year one Thousand eight Hundred and _thirty two_
By me _Wm Purcell_

This Marriage was solemnized between us ⎰ _Hugh Butler_
⎱ _Ellen McClean_

In the Presence of ⎰ _John Davies_
⎱ _Edward Stephens Kinsman_

No. _4_

Thomas Nowlyn, Clonee of _the_ Parish _of the Union of Inch and Killgorman farm_
and _Sarah Gilbert, Ballygarbin_ of _the_ Parish _of the Union of Inch & Killgorman_
were married in this _Church_ by _Licence_ with Consent of _Father_ this _Twenty Second_ Day of _March_ in the Year one Thousand eight Hundred and _thirty four_
By me _Aaron King_

This Marriage was solemnized between us ⎰ _Thomas Nowlan_
⎱ _Sarah Silvester_ her X Mark

In the Presence of ⎰ _John Daniel_
⎱ _Thomas Gilbert_

No. _5_

Patrick Dillon, Ballyellin of _the_ Parish _of Inch, Laborer_
and _Hannah Feeney, Ballyellin_ of _the_ Parish _of Inch_
were married in this _Church_ by _Banns_ with Consent of _Eliza Kinch_ this _Twenty seventh_ Day of _October_ in the Year one Thousand eight Hundred and _thirty four_
By me _B.H. Mooney - Curate_

This Marriage was solemnized between us ⎰ _Patrick Dillon_
⎱ _Hannah Feeney_

In the Presence of ⎰ _John Daniel_
⎱ _Eliza_ her X Mark _Kinch_

No. _6_

8 *Church of Ireland marriage register entries for 1832 and 1834*

Although the original bonds were destroyed in 1922, some abstracts do exist and are useful for establishing the intended place of marriage, the name of the second surety, the couple's places of residence and the approximate date of the ceremony, as the date of the bond will be only a few days beforehand. Marriage Bond Indexes are housed in the PRO and are arranged by diocese, although none exist for Derry and very few for Ardfert, while those for Limerick survive only for the year 1844. Indexes give the couple's names, the year of marriage and the parish in which it was scheduled to take place.

Special licences

These were issued by the Prerogative Court of Armagh (PCA) the seat of the Primate of Ireland and the equivalent of the Prerogative Court of Canterbury. It is not certain why special licences were used, but it appears to have been largely for snobbish reasons, as they were fairly costly to obtain and the majority were taken out by wealthy Dubliners.

Abstracts giving details of the ceremony and parish are to be found in the Genealogical Office in Dublin's Kildare Street.

It is important to bear in mind that banns and licences are only a record of intent to marry and are not proof that the ceremony ever actually took place.

Mixed marriages

Throughout history there have been instances of love triumphing over religious differences and Ireland has had its share of such marriages, between Catholics and Protestants, although even today it is a practice frowned upon by both communities.

Until the 1840s, a mixed marriage, if it were to be legal, had to be performed by an Anglican clergyman. Although marriage bonds were not issued for either Catholic or Non-Conformist weddings, presumably on the assumption that they were not important enough, they were frequently entered into in the case of a Catholic marrying an Anglican and so should be traceable in the Indexes in the PRO.

Once a C of I wedding entry has been located, a Catholic wedding should be searched for, if the relevant register exists. This is likely to have taken place a few days prior to the Protestant one, as the latter was usually considered invalid by the Catholics

143

involved and was only undergone to make the marriage acceptable in the eyes of the law.

Marriage certificates

All non-Catholic marriages were, as we have already seen, supposed to have been registered civilly after 1st April 1845, although many slipped through the registrar's net.

Information appearing on Irish marriage certificates includes: the names of the couple; their age (usually 'full' or 'minor'); their addresses and occupations; and their fathers' names and occupations.

Death in Ireland

Irish Death Certificates list: the place where the death occurred; the age, which, by the way, is often incorrect; the occupation of the deceased; marital status and the name of the informant. No mention is made of spouse, children or, in the case of a woman, the maiden name.

In the General Registrar's Office in Dublin, deaths at sea as certified by British consuls abroad 1864–1921 and in the Army, throughout the British Empire 1864–1921, may be consulted; there is also an Index of Irish soldiers in the Boer War 1899–1902.

In the Library of the Society of Genealogists in London are *Ireland's Memorial Books 1914–18*; these are in 8 volumes and include both Army and Navy personnel, with a list of names including number, rank, regiment and the place where the serviceman was born and where he died.

The above sources prove that many thousands of Irishmen and women fought bravely and loyally for Britain in her many wars; in addition to these are the Irish people who died away from home, most of them immigrants, but some killed in accidents while doing temporary or seasonal work, usually in England.

Wakes

> They wrapped him up in a nice clean sheet,
> And laid him out upon the bed,
> With a gallon of whiskey at this feet,
> And a barrel of porter at his head.
> His friends assembled at the wake,

And Mrs Finnegan called for lunch,
First they brought in tay and cakes,
Then pipes, tobacco and whiskey punch.

Fortunately Finnegan's Wake, which 'happened' in the 1850s, was a little premature as the chief participant was only stunned from falling off a ladder, while 'full'. He was later brought back to life again by the accidental but effective external application of his native beverage.

In the *National Geographic Magazine*'s coverage of the Celts (Vol. 151, No. 5, May 1977) a funeral in the Aran Islands is described. The writer, an American, half-expected the carousing which he had heard might last a full week if taking place in Co. Clare; or there might be drinking, singing, horseplay or dancing with the corpse to give the deceased a send-off which would be truly unforgettable. Instead, there was soft candle-light and quiet conversation, although the room was crowded. The corpse 'sat propped up primly in bed, night-capped and gloved, hands crossed' and was kept company until dawn, when tea was served and the neighbours left the house. At the burial itself there was no keening or other dramatic behaviour, only a procession of villagers paying their last respects to their old friend.

Catholic burial records

When an Irishman died away from his ancestral parish, his body was likely to be brought back for interment in the family graveyard if this were at all practical. Catholics, as well as other non-Anglicans, were buried in the village graveyard, even if this were attached to a Protestant church. Because the C of I was the Established Church until 1869, all villagers were entitled to be buried in its churchyard, so it is worth searching such places and their registers, even if it is absolutely certain that the ancestor in question was a Catholic. Anglican clergymen, unlike the law, were fairly tolerant in their dealings with their Catholic neighbours and usually treated all burials alike in this respect.

As always, one must remember that burials were not automatically recorded in Catholic registers; neither, on the whole, were deaths, so research in Anglican registers is a must.

About 2% of Catholic parishes do have burial records dating from the eighteenth century, and relatively extensive ones exist for the diocese of Ardagh, Clonmacnoise, Dromore, Elphin, Ferns (sometimes giving the age of the deceased) and Meath, only. No pre-1880 burial records exist for Cloyne, Cork, Ross and Tuam dioceses.

Protestant burial records

Unlike Catholic registers, C of I ones do list burials, not only of Anglicans, but also of Catholics, Presbyterians and Methodists. In most parishes Catholic burials could well be in the majority, owing to the high percentage of Catholics compared with Protestants in Ireland.

Memorial inscriptions

As in England, it is comparatively rare in graveyards to find gravestones or tombs which date from before the mid-eighteenth century. Inside churches, of course, monuments and memorials abound but, like the survivors outside in the elements, they are mainly to the middle and upper classes, who could afford such durable souvenirs of their existence on earth. The labouring classes, if they were commemorated at all, had simple wooden crosses or inscriptions, which were soon destroyed by the wind and rain. In Ireland, many people would have been buried hastily, without even a coffin, for fear of contagion, especially in the mid-nineteenth century.

This is most unfortunate because, in the almost total absence of burial entries apart from the late-starting C of I ones, memorial inscriptions are of great importance; furthermore, Irish grave-stones, where they do exist, can prove very valuable aids to family history research, as it is by no means uncommon for them to commemorate up to four generations – a real treasure trove for those lucky enough to encounter them.

Another type of memorial and one not generally encountered in Britain, is the placing of enamel plaques on the end of church pews. They are inscribed with something similar to 'Pray for the Soul of . . .' and the date of death. Since the end of the last century, transcriptions of memorials have been made by the Association for the Preservation of the Memorials of the Dead in Ireland. The Assocation's Journal, which runs to some twelve volumes, records more than 10,000 inscriptions collected from all over the country.

Name.	Abode.	When buried.	Age.	By whom the Ceremony was performed.
John Daniel No. 1	Coolgreny	8th Novemr. 1860	27 years	Gibson Black Rector &c
John Lchee No. 139	Inch School House	27th Novemr 1860	8 days	Gibson Black Rector &c
Moses Godkin No. 139	Kilcavan	10th Decemr 1860	84 Years	Gibson Black at Kilgorman
Stephen Cuthbert No. 140	Clonevanny	27th Decemr 1860	6 Years	Gibson Black Rector &c
William Brush Black No.	Inch Rectory	24th December 1861	20 years	Rev Richd Eakins Curate of Gorey
James Hempenstatt (chat) No. 142	Ashwood	1st January 1862	71 Years	Gibson Black Rector &c
Ruth Canning No. 143	Constabulary Station Coolgreny	25th February 1862	34 Years	Gibson Black Rector &c
Gibson Erwyn Black No. 144	Inch Rectory	8th April 1862	Three months 11 days	Gibson Black Rector &c

9 *Burial register entries, 1860–1862*

The Library of the Genealogical Office holds a complete set; transcription lists have been compiled for Cos. Wexford and Wicklow, and the Ulster Historical Foundation, Belfast, has published twenty-five volumes of pre-1900 inscriptions for Belfast, Down and Antrim.

Irish wills

Unfortunately there is no easy way of locating an Irish will; neither is there one central repository which contains all known surviving wills, many having been destroyed. The place where the researcher would be best advised to begin is the PRO, where records of wills fall into three main groups.

1. Pre-1858 wills

Before 1858 wills were proved in Church of Ireland diocesan courts. Unhappily, the actual wills have been destroyed, but indexes to many, giving the name of the testator and the date the will was proved, may be consulted in the Reading Room of the PRO. When the deceased had property in more than one diocese, the will was proved by the Prerogative Court of Armagh (the PCA) instead of the diocesan one, between the years 1536 and 1810, and are listed in the Betham Papers, which are Sir William Betham's notebooks. Vicars's *Index to Prerogative Wills, 1536–1810* is also available in the Reading Room.

In 1897 Sir Arthur Vicars set about compiling an index to the abstracts which Sir William Betham had already made into the 39 volumes now housed in the Public Record Office in Dublin, or National Archives, as it is now known. These abstracts formed the basis of what Betham called his 'genealogical analyses', which took the form of charts, now in the Genealogical Office, Dublin. A mere quarter-century after Sir Arthur had made his Index came the destruction of virtually all the original wills in the fire at the Four Courts.

The Index contains some 40,000 entries, in alphabetical order, under the name of the testator, and giving rank, and usually occupation, county and town of residence, and the year in which probate was granted. Naturally, being only an index, no idea is given as to the actual contents of the original wills, information so valuable where it survives. The 1897 edition of Sir Arthur Vicars's work was reissued by the Genealogical Publishing Co. Inc., in 1989.

Only eleven wills proved by the PCA, and a solitary specimen from Dublin Consistorial Court, have survived. There is also a small number of pre-1858 will books in the PRO.

2. Post-1858 wills

After 1858 wills were proved either in the principal registry in Dublin, or in district registries. In the PRO Reading Room is a calendar of all wills proved since 1858. The volumes are arranged by surname, in alphabetical order, and include the name, address and date of the testator, together with the value of the estate, and the names and addresses of the executors. There is a volume for each year, with a consolidated index 1858–77.

3. Wills not housed in the Public Record Office

In the PRO Reading Room is a card index of wills not actually held there, but known to exist elsewhere. The most common places where such wills are to be found are among family and estate papers, and those belonging to solicitors.

The PRO produces a leaflet, 'Calendar of Wills and Administrations'. The Reports of the Deputy Keeper of Public Records (in particular the 55th, 56th and 57th Reports) mention several thousand wills; copies are in the PRO itself, and also in the National Library of Ireland.

In the eighteenth century, many Irish wills were registered along with deeds. Abstracts have been made from such wills, and run to two large printed volumes, covering the years 1708–1787. These are usually known as Eustace's Will Abstracts (properly the Irish Manuscripts Commission's *Registry of Deeds, Abstracts of Wills*, edited by P. B. Eustace), and a printed index is kept in the Genealogical Office, Kildare Street.

Finally, do not forget to try mainland British repositories such as Somerset House, the Public Record Office of Scotland, Scottish Sheriff Courts, and English and Welsh County Record Offices, as appropriate, if the ancestor is likely to have made a will in England, Wales or Scotland, having land or property both there and in Ireland.

8

VISITING IRELAND

Sooner or later, anyone seriously engaged in researching their Irish ancestry will want to visit the country for themselves, grateful as they might have been for outside help. Even if they have had little success in tracing their family as individuals, they will wish to see the country, if not the actual place where their forebears once lived, and will no longer be content with charts and maps and photographs.

As has already been stated, it is impossible to put too much preparation into your efforts before you leave home. Time in Ireland will be short, and there are bound to be many distractions offered by the modern Irish, too many opportunities to enjoy yourself without once looking at any sources of family history.

Furthermore, there are bound to be certain aspects of Irish life with which you will be unfamiliar, even if you have spent some time in Britain and have read all the right travel guides. It is also as well to bear in mind the fact that slight differences exist between Britain and Ireland, unimportant as they might seem to a holiday-maker, which might detract from your success – like, for example, public holidays, when the repository which you have travelled thousands of miles to visit will certainly be closed.

Public holidays

Public holidays in the Republic are similar to those in Britain, but they are not identical. They consist of:

New Year 1st January
St Patrick's Day 17th March
Good Friday (not an official holiday but generally observed as one)
Easter Monday
June Holiday First Monday in June
August Holiday First Monday in August
October Holiday Last Monday in October

Christmas Day
St Stephen's Day 26th December
Christmas Holiday 27th December

In the Six Counties of Northern Ireland public holidays are the same as in Britain, apart from there being no August Bank Holiday; this is replaced by the first Monday in September. In addition, there is a holiday on Battle of the Boyne Day, 12th July, which commemorates the victory of William of Orange's army over that of James II, in 1690.

For non-Britons, incidentally, the public holidays in England and Wales are:

New Year 1st January
Good Friday
Easter Monday
May Day or the nearest Monday to it
Late Spring Bank Holiday in late May
Summer Bank Holiday in late August
Christmas Day
Boxing Day 26th December

In Scotland the New Year Holiday is kept a day or two later than in England and Wales, and the Summer Bank Holiday falls early in August, not at the end.

Business hours

Irish business premises generally open from 9.30 a.m. until 5.30 p.m. although in Dublin most open at 9 a.m.

Banks open on Mondays to Fridays from 10 a.m. until 12.30 p.m. and 1.30 p.m. until 3 p.m., shorter hours than their British counterparts, although most Dublin banks stay open until 5 p.m. on Thursdays.

Some towns have Early Closing Days which will alter from place to place, and most shops will close for lunch.

Currency

The Irish Punt or Pound, which is written IR£, is divided into 100 pence. The coins come in the same denomination as in Britain, except that there is no £1 coin in the Republic. The shape, colour, and size of the Irish 50p, 10p, 5p, 2p and 1p coins are identical to their British counterparts, only the 20p being distinctive, although, of course, the designs on them are different.

British currency is valid in the Republic and will be readily accepted, although the two Pounds are not on a par, and anyone spending sterling will lose money, for it is stronger than the IR£. While it may be convenient to hand over a 10p coin for a postcard, travellers are otherwise advised to change their money at banks and bureaux de change (£1 coins are not generally accepted in Irish shops). Most credit cards are accepted, certainly all of those which carry the Eurocard symbol; for encashment and payment of personal cheques, a Eurocard is essential.

Those Britons wishing to order photocopies of documents, or to purchase publications from the PRO in Dublin, may be interested to learn that the PRO accepts sterling cheques through the post, made out at face value, pound for pound.

Overseas visitors should note that Irish currency, similar as it may be, is not valid in the United Kingdom, even in Northern Ireland and, unless you are prepared to pay bank commission when it is changed for sterling like any other currency, it is a good idea to spend it in Ireland. Banks in Britain will only change Irish notes, not coins, so try to avoid bringing a large amount into the country.

In the Six Counties of Northern Ireland, the use of sterling is standard as elsewhere in Britain, the only difference in the coins being the Northern Irish £1 coin in circulation there. Banks in Northern Ireland open the usual 10 a.m. to 3.30 p.m. as in the rest of the country, except that they close for lunch from 12.30 until 1.30 p.m.

Tourist boards and their publications

The Tourist Board of the Republic, Bord Fáilte (or Welcome Board) has branches all over Ireland and in the major European and North American cities. Two of its main offices are:

PO Box 1083
Dublin 8

and

150 New Bond Street
London W1Y 0AQ

Bord Fáilte issue a series of publications covering an assortment of subjects: Accommodation and Catering; Hotels and Guesthouses; Caravanning and Camping; Dining Out; Self-Catering; Farmhouses; Town and Country Homes. It also produces:

Guides: the whole Republic, plus 26 individual county guides.

Maps: the whole Republic, plus North, West, East and South Holiday Maps.

Posters: a series ranging from cottages to doorways.

There is also a yearly brochure, the Traveller's Guide, which gives up-to-the minute information and suggestions for holidays.

The Northern Ireland Tourist Board's Head Office is at:

River House
48 High Street
Belfast BT1 2DS

with major offices in Europe, North America and, of course, London and Dublin.

The N.I.T.B. also offers a series of booklets and guides, most of which are available in the reference section of British public libraries, or from the Tourist Board itself.

The Irish Press

It is worth considering approaching an Irish newspaper with a view to placing an advertisement for information about your ancestors, if you have sufficient information to warrant doing so. Or, better still, why not write a letter asking for advice and contacts and ask for it to be printed in their correspondence column or, if you feel so inclined, suggest they interview you for an article in the paper; a good opening for you, and good copy for them!

The addresses and telephone numbers of leading national and provincial newspapers, both in the Republic and in Northern Ireland, may be found in the telephone directory's Golden Pages and Yellow Pages respectively. Those listed below are among the most important.

Dublin

Independent Newspapers Ltd.
90 Abbey Street Middle,
Dublin I (telephone 73 16 66)

Irish Press plc,
Tara Street,
Dublin 2 (telephone 71 33 33)

Irish Times,
10 D'Olier Street,
Dublin 2 (telephone 79 20 22)

Galway

Galway Observer Company
 Ltd.,
Olde Malte Mall,
High Street,
Galway (telephone 6 30 13)

Limerick

Limerick Leader Ltd.,
54 O'Connell Street,
Limerick (telephone 31 52 33)

Cork

Cork Examiner,
95 Patrick Street,
Cork (telephone 96 33 00)

Irish Times,
2 MacCurtain Street,
Cork (telephone 50 91 97)

Belfast

Belfast Telegraph,
124 Royal Avenue,
Belfast (telephone 321242)

Irish Times Ltd.,
110 Great Victoria Street,
Belfast (telephone 323379)

The Irish Catholic Directory

Easily overlooked as a reference book, particularly by Protestant researchers, the *Directory* lists Ireland's clergy (by name, unfortunately) its parishes under diocese, its archbishops and bishops and also Catholic ones in England, Wales and Scotland.

Apart from the Catholic information which one might expect to find therein, the *Directory* also lists other Christian churches in Ireland.

The advertisements are not to be missed, for they give a picture of Catholic Ireland today which might not be over-apparent to an outsider who may assume that such merchandise is a figment of the novelist's imagination. Favourites seem Candle Suppliers, Clerical Tailors, whose goods include 'tonsure shirts', and Lourdes Tours.

The Irish Catholic Directory is published annually and may be found outside Ireland in large British central reference libraries.

Electoral lists

Those people who are entitled to vote in elections are listed on electoral lists which are displayed in all Irish post offices. The lists include everyone of voting age (eighteen and over) who is normally resident in the area and they are compiled under townlands. In Ireland names can still be an important indicator as to where a family could have been living a century, or perhaps more, ago. Of course any names of the family under research who are listed should not be ignored for they may well prove excellent contacts.

In England the local Electoral Rolls, including thousands of Irish people on them, are to be found most easily in local libraries.

Solicitors

Try to establish if your family may have had, or still has, a solicitor back home in Ireland. Wills, or other official and valuable documents, may yield clues. Irish solicitors are more likely to retain clients' personal papers than their English or Welsh colleagues for several reasons, the chief of which are the absence of County Record Offices where important documents may be safely lodged for posterity, together with the closeness of Irish communities where generations of professional men, such as solicitors and doctors, would have handled the business and welfare of generations of the same family. Thus everybody would come to have a fair idea of everyone else's affairs.

Existing family trees

Try to establish, preferably before arriving in Ireland, if a family tree has ever been compiled or, better still, printed, for the name which you are about to research. Obviously there is better access to this sort of information in Ireland than elsewhere and repositories and local libraries should be approached. Although it may be unlikely that there is any direct connection, do not dismiss out of hand ties to a great family. Having traced a ready-made pedigree, keep a copy, for this just could provide a lead to a lesser-known branch to which you might belong.

Through the years many families have experienced periodic rises and falls in their fortunes and 'claiming kin' with one of the great families may not be such a high-flown idea. Conversely, beware of those who believe, and try to persuade you, that with enough persistence and ingenuity a link can be proved with a famous person of the same name. Go ahead if you really believe there could be a genuine connection, but do not deceive yourself into thinking so if there is no sound basis for it.

Organized researching in Ireland

Some family history societies arrange trips to other areas, even other countries, to enable their members to travel together and share advice and experiences. North American societies travel across the Atlantic to do research in Britain and Ireland, splitting up when they arrive here in order to go to their individual ancestral homelands. Make enquiries as to whether your own local society, or one that a fellow-member has heard about, is arranging such a visit to Ireland. If they are, join it; if not, how about organizing your own?

Aer Lingus, Ireland's national airline, offers an 'Irish Heritage' package, which includes both 'air and land arrangements' as they put it, plus the services of the Irish Genealogical Research Society whose members are prepared to

do the groundwork in finding your ancestors, then give you a map showing those places important in your family's history. All can be tailored to your particular needs, time available and budget. Book through Aer Lingus or travel agents.

The quotation is from *Frommer's Ireland on $30 a Day* by Susan Poole, published by Prentice Hall, New York 1987. Unfortunately, it is not as easy as it sounds there and, naturally enough, even the experts at the Irish Genealogical Society cannot work miracles if the information which you give them is not sufficient, so be warned. If you know what you are doing and have enough details to make such a trip worthwhile the result may be excellent, but never rely on anyone else, however experienced, to do the groundwork for you.

The Bord Fáilte brochure, which appears each year, lists events, some of which may well appeal to the amateur family historian. Among the 1987–88 examples were:

Kilkenny Genealogical Circle Roots Weekend Workshop in October, details:
Mr Pat Nolan,
College Road,
Kilkenny

and

US Origins Roots and Family Name Seminars,
Club House Hotel,
Patrick Street,
Kilkenny.
Once again contact Mr Pat Nolan at the above address.

Dr James Ryan, author of the very useful *Guide to Tracing your Dublin Ancestors* (Flyleaf Press, 4 Spencer Villas, Glenageary, Co. Dublin) and *Irish Records – Sources for Family and Local History* (published by Ancestry Inc., Salt Lake City) has set up a series of practical Irish family history courses. The first ones are scheduled for the autumn of 1989.

The 5-day programme, based in Dublin, will concentrate on Irish records and their use and include visits to principal archives. The course should prove of value both to those wishing to trace their own families and to professional researchers. As well as practical sessions, students will attend lectures on the social history of Ireland, with emphasis on the eighteenth and nineteenth centuries as well as on the country's major holdings of source material.

Although it is as yet early days to speculate as to the future of such a course, one hopes it will become a regular feature of Irish family history study. The Course Administrator is:

Mr Brendan Wafer,
Stratford House,
Barnhill Road,
Dalkey,
Co. Dublin
Telephone (011) 353-1-857731

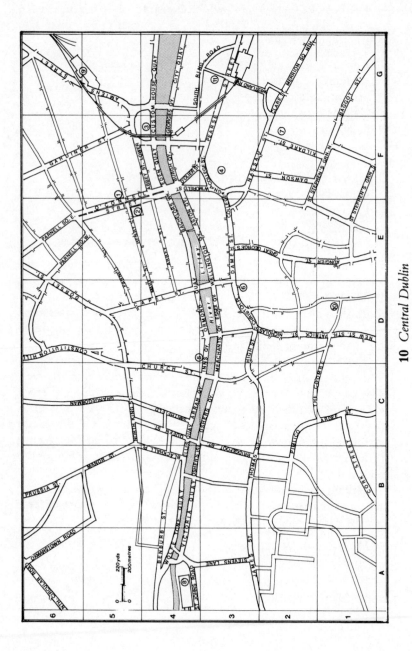

10 *Central Dublin*

KEY TO MAP OF DUBLIN

1 Tourist Information Office, O'Connell Street (E4)
2 General Post Office, O'Connell Street (E4)
3 Custom House, Bus Station and Airport Terminus, Store Street (E4)
4 Trinity College, College Green East (E3)
5 The Four Courts, Inns Quay (C4)
6 Dublin Castle, Dame Street (D3)
7 National Library, Leinster House and National Museum, Kildare Street, National Art Gallery, Merrion Street (E3)
8 Heuston Station (Kingsbridge) (B4)
9 Connolly Station (Amiens Street) (F5)
10 Marsh's Library, Patrick Street (D3)
11 Joyce House, 8–11 Lombard Street East (F3)

What's where in Ireland — a resumé

Dublin

Genealogical Office, Kildare Street (formerly in Dublin Castle)
Open Monday to Friday 9.30 a.m. to 5 p.m. No admission charge. Includes:

Heraldic Museum
Pedigrees of many Irish families
A Copy of Primary (or Griffith's) Valuations
Eustace's Will Abstracts and printed index to Eustace Collection of Wills.
Complete set of the *Journal of the Assocation for the Preservation of the Memorials of the Dead in Ireland*.

General Register Office (Oifig an Ard-Chláraitheora) Joyce House, 8–11 Lombard Street East, Dublin 2 (telephone 01 711000). Open Monday to Friday 9.30 a.m. to 12.30 p.m. and 2.15 p.m. to 4.30 p.m.

Contrary to what is often read about the fate of Irish records no *civil* (as opposed to church) records were lost in 1922 during the fire at the Custom House, for the good reason that they were not even housed there at this period, being then at Charlemont House, now the Municipal Gallery of Modern Art. It was not until 1929 that the GRO moved into the Custom House where it remained until December 1983, when it moved to its present home, Joyce House, a spacious, modern office block.

Contents:

General Entries of Births, Marriages and Deaths 1864 to 1921 (for Northern Ireland) and to the present day for the Republic.

Most Non-Catholic Marriages 1845 onwards

Births and Deaths of Irish Residents 1864 to 1921 as registered by British Consuls abroad.

The General Register Office has Indexes which researchers may search for themselves and the Search Rooms have staff on hand to give assistance. The Index Books are arranged in quarters of the year and start in 1878.

A limited search over 5 years costs IR£1 (1987 price), with an unlimited general search costing IR£11.

Photocopies of Certificates are available to take away, unlike the several weeks' wait to be expected in London. Each copy costs IR£1.50

The National Archives, formerly *The Public Record Office of Ireland*, Four Courts, Dublin 1 (01 733833). Open Monday to Friday 10 a.m. to 5 p.m. Note: no documents are produced between 12.45 and 2 p.m. Please address all correspondence to the Deputy Keeper.

The Four Courts date from the time when Grattan was Prime Minister of Ireland, prior to the Union in 1801. They were started in 1785 to a design by Thomas Cooley and extended by James Gandon and were opened for use as courtrooms in 1796. During the Civil War they were badly damaged but have now been reconstructed and feature largely among Dublin's historic buildings.

The Public Record Office has a search room with a card index, open to the public. Among its chief treasures of interest to family historians are:

Census Returns: 1901 and 1911, plus a few earlier survivors
Primary (or Griffith's) Valuations 1847 to 1865
Tithe Applotment Books: for all Irish counties 1823 to 1837

Protestant Marriage Licence Bonds: 1750 to 1845
Convert Rolls
Parish Registers: microfilm copies of many Church of Ireland
    registers up to 1870
Wills
    Some existing originals
    Abstracts from all Prerogative Court of Armagh (PCA) wills
      to 1800
Index to wills up to 1858
    Calendar of wills and administrations 1858 onwards
    Vicars' Index to Prerogative Wills 1536 to 1810
    Wills proved since 1904
    Sir William Betham's notebooks on wills 1536 to 1810.

NOTE The Public Record Office of Ireland now calls itself the National Archives. The former name, PROI, has been used throughout this book to avoid confusion as this is the title under which it has been listed in bibliographies, catalogues etc.

The National Library and Archives, Kildare Street, Dublin 2 (telephone 01 765521)
Open Monday to Thursday 10 a.m. to 9 p.m. Friday 10 a.m. to 5 p.m. Saturday 10 a.m. to 1 p.m.
In addition to some 14,000 manuscript volumes, which include a vast amount of material of interest to family historians, the Library and Archives contain:

Primary (Griffith's) Valuations
Newspapers on Microfilm
Most pre 1800 Roman Catholic Parish Registers on film (Note:
    written permission may be needed from the relevant Bishop
    before access is given)
Most post 1830 Catholic Registers on film
Trade Directories, Journals, Newspapers and similar material.

Registry of Deeds, King's Inn, Henrietta Street (off Bolton Street), Dublin 1 (telephone 01 748911)
Open Monday to Friday 10 a.m. to 4.30 p.m. Charge of IR£1 per day for research.
Records date from 1708 and mainly concern the gentry and professional classes, although not exclusively so.

Holdings include:

Deeds, Leases, Business Transactions
Marriage Licences
Wills.

There are Surname and Place-name indexes and copies of documents are available for a fee of about IR£1 each. These are not immediately obtainable, but will be sent through the post.

Representative Church Body Library, Braemor Park, Dublin 14
Generally referred to as the R.C.B.L. this body holds many Church of Ireland original Parish Registers, particularly where the parish no longer exists or has been combined with another parish. It also has lists of Church of Ireland parishes in the Republic whose registers have been microfilmed by the Public Record Office of Northern Ireland in Belfast.

Society of Friends, Friends' Meeting House, Eustace Street, Dublin (telephone 01 778088)
Historical Library open Thursday mornings 10 a.m. to 1 p.m.
　The Library contains:

Birth, Marriage and Death registers
Six volumes of seventeenth- and eighteenth-century Quaker wills
Personal writings of Friends.
Minute books of meetings
Manuscript pedigrees
Details of relief work carried out during the Famine.

State Paper Office, Birmingham Tower, Dublin Castle, Dublin 2 (telephone 01 792777 ext. 2518)
Another historic building, the State Paper Office is the only portion of the thirteenth-century Dublin Castle to survive. The Office houses those records which, before independence, belonged to the Chief Secretary for Ireland's Office, among which are:

Details of convicts and their sentences
Details of transportation and penal servitude (particularly to Australia)
Papers concerning the rebellion of 1798

162

Proceedings of the Dublin Society of United Irishmen
Fenian and Land League records
Proceedings of the Evicted Tenants Commission.

Belfast

Belfast Linen Hall Library, 7 Donegall Square North, Belfast 1
(telephone 249156) Yet another historic building, dating from
1788.
    The Library is particularly strong in its manuscript collection
relating to local families and their transactions. Also included are:

Published genealogies
Birth, Marriage and Death indexes up to 1800 as taken from
    insertions in the *Belfast Newsletter*
The Blackwood Collection, being volumes of pedigrees,
    chiefly from Co. Down and Belfast itself.

Irish Genealogical Association, 164 Kingsway, Dunmurry, Belfast
BT17 9AD (telephone 629595)
    The Association offers advance research for those who wish to
come to Ireland later and continue with the thrill of the chase for
themselves. Alternatively, researchers can be found to help, or
tours arranged to travel 'in the steps of your ancestors'.

Presbyterian Historical Society, Church House, Fisherwick Place,
Belfast
    The Society holds the following:

Presbyterian Baptism and Marriage records dating back to the
    seventeenth century.
Copies of the 1775 Religious Census organised by the Church
List of Protestant householders in the year 1775
The Religious Census of 1766
Certificates of Transference between Presbyterian
    congregations.

The Public Record Office of Northern Ireland, 66 Balmoral Avenue, BT9
6YN (telephone 661621)
The Northern Irish PRO produces an excellent series of short
guides to sources which it holds, with a separate booklet for each

of the Six Counties. The PRONI's most important contents include:

Microfilm copies of Church of Ireland and Presbyterian Parish Registers for the six counties

Subsidy Rolls 1662–68, being lists of both Protestant 'Planters' and native Irish, with their parishes of residence

Wills

Land Records, Deeds and Leases

Marriage Settlements and Family Notes

Card Index to pedigrees held.

The Ulster Historical Foundation, 68 Balmoral Avenue, Belfast BT9 6NY (telephone 681365)

This non-profit-making organisation may be called the genealogical branch of the PRONI. Established in 1957, its aim is to stimulate an interest in the genealogy and history of the Province and to publicize source material of interest to the Ulster family historian.

The Foundation helps individuals with specific enquiries about their personal ancestry by means of a research service. Initial registration costs about £15, which is not returnable. In addition, the average search and report fee costs about £80, depending on the information given to the Foundation initially and the amount of time and trouble involved in producing a result. The Foundation will not accept a commission unless its researchers are reasonably sure that it will prove successful.

Preliminary research is offered and is not likely to cost more than £14; all prices are as quoted in 1986. As the searches, of which there are about 300 each year, are carried out in strict rotation, there is likely to be a waiting period of at least a year before work can begin, therefore work cannot, under any circumstances, be undertaken while the client is in Ireland awaiting further results.

The Foundation issues a series of volumes: on pre-1900 gravestone inscriptions, with work still in progress; on emigration to Colonial America; on the Plantation of Ulster; on the Penal Era; on Scottish-Irish Relations; and also biographies of famous Ulstermen.

The Ulster Genealogical and Historical Guild, under the auspices of the Foundation, brings together subscribers with similar interests. Its annual newsletter contains articles on Ulster and Irish genealogy and history, together with a Guild Subscribers' Interest List which also appears yearly and probably offers the most complete record available of Ulster research in progress.

The Registrar-General's Office of Northern Ireland, Oxford House, 49–55 Chichester Street, Belfast BT1 4HL (telephone 235211) The Office houses:

> Returns of Births, Marriages and Deaths in the Province from Partition in 1921 onwards.
>
> Census Returns for 1931 and 1951, none being taken in 1941 due to the War; for pre-Partition surviving Returns, generally only 1901 and 1911, see Dublin.

The system used in the Belfast Registrar-General's Office is similar to that in Dublin except that *admission is by appointment only*, owing to lack of space. A full-day search of the indexes costs £4.25 (1986). There is no photocopying service available.

Heritage centres and folk parks

Local Heritage Centres

The Centres were established as a result of the economic recession, when the Irish State Training Agency made use of the manpower available in the form of unemployed young people to restore old buildings. These were afterwards turned into what were in effect museums of local social history. While the men did the actual building, the girls were given training in appropriate techniques in order that they might be able to carry out surveys and index records.

Much of this sort of work has actually been accomplished but unfortunately, in some cases, the output has proved to be on a very small scale and is frequently not made available to the ordinary researcher. A further drawback to what would at first sight seem to be a godsend to family historians is the fact that those people who compile any index can claim copyright on it.

The indexes produced by this venture are really transcripts arranged in alphabetical order and normally include the whole of the record indexed.

To give an example of the work carried out at a Local Heritage Centre, let us cite the one at Corofin, near Ennis in Co. Clare. It indexed all the Roman Catholic records up until 1900 and then went on to index all of the Irish 'Big Four' sources (church records, Griffith's Primary Valuation, Tithe Applotment Books and existing Census Returns) plus other sources relevant to that part of Ireland. In addition, the Clare Centre offers a research service.

Like the one at Corofin, some Centres arrange displays showing various aspects of local life over the years, while the Leitrim Centre at Ballinamore is housed in the County Library and offers a full-time professional service, charging fees according to estimates which will be sent on request; payment is required in advance.

Folk parks

While not dealing with ancestral research on a personal level, Ireland's folk parks go a long way towards explaining how one's ancestors might have lived and worked over the centuries. Both the one in the Republic, in the grounds of Bunratty Castle near the Shannon Airport development, and the Ulster-American Folk Park, in County Tyrone, are famous world-wide.

Bunratty Folk Park stands beside the busy main road between Limerick City and Shannon International Airport, which only enhances the feeling of remoteness from the twentieth century, once one enters the grounds of the castle.

In the 1960s the nucleus of the Park, its first reed-thatched cottage, was built and since then it has acquired a selection of typically Irish dwellings. These range from the home of a well-to-do farmer from Co. Limerick, down to the humblest of labourers' huts. The eighteenth and nineteenth centuries are particularly well represented. Not only are there houses from the immediate area, there is also a farmhouse from the Golden Vale of Tipperary and buildings from all over south-west Ireland, some of course being typical of the country as a whole. An additional feature is a complete nineteenth-century Irish town with shops, Post Office, printing-works and even a flour mill operated by a water wheel.

Overlooking the folk park is the Talbot Collection of Agricultural Machines, housed in the farm courtyard of Georgian Bunratty House. Some machines are old favourites, others may prove unrecognizable.

An excellent guide-book to Bunratty Castle, the folk park and the Talbot Collection is obtainable from Shannon Free Airport Development Company Ltd, Shannon Free Airport, Co. Clare.

The guide contains information of a social and economic nature concerning the history of this part of Ireland, as well as being a souvenir.

The Ulster-American Folk Park, Camphill, Omagh, Co. Tyrone (telephone Omagh 3292–3) is open daily from 11 a.m. to 6.30 p.m. During the winter months (October to April) it closes at 4.30 p.m. The park opens on Sundays in summer from 11.30 to 7 p.m.

Midway between Omagh and Newtownstewart, the focal point of the park is the cottage (now belonging to the National Trust) from which Thomas Mellon emigrated in his fifth year to the United States in 1818. Mellon was destined to become a judge, a banker and the father of Andrew Mellon, the statesman and developer of Pittsburgh, as well as a great art collector. The Park was created with money donated for the purpose by the Mellon family, with a view to showing how life in both Ulster and America would have been in the seventeenth and eighteenth centuries.

There are Old and New World sections. The Old World has a meeting-house, school, smithy and shop, while the New features a stockade with covered waggons, the Mellon log cabin at Turtle Creek, Pennsylvania and farm buildings. There is a farm museum and viewpoint, as well as an exhibition centre showing the story of emigration from Northern Ireland to America.

The Scotch-Irish Trust of Ulster, also at Camphill, was established in 1967 thanks to an endowment from the Mellon family. Their ancestor, the above-mentioned Thomas, lived nearby in a farmhouse which his American descendants have restored in his memory. The trust carries out educational research work in the field of Scottish-Irish connections with America, as well as maintaining the folk park as one of the highlights of a trip 'home' for Ulster-Americans.

CONCLUSION: THE FUTURE OF IRISH FAMILY HISTORY RESEARCH

Until the mid-1980s, the researcher had no choice but to travel to Dublin or Belfast for all of his or her requirements and with only a fifty-fifty chance of success at that. The majority of queries which arise concern events which took place in the period prior to the introduction of full Civil Registration in 1864 and necessarily involve the use of church records.

Most of the registers consulted are Roman Catholic and if one needs to consult those kept before 1880 one would be able to do so either in the original, or on microfilm in the National Library of Ireland. For events taking place before 1880, apart from church records, one would need to see Griffith's Valuation records and then the Tithe Applotment Books, to ascertain the likely whereabouts of one's family at a given time. The originals of both sets of records and the first copies made, are in the Irish capitals; although the British Library also has a set, access is difficult for the majority of British people even if they manage to acquire a Reader's Ticket. In short, widely distributed copies and transcripts of leading Irish sources for family historians were desperately needed.

Unlike England and Wales which have County Record Offices or Archives, plus other repositories for the larger cities and boroughs, Ireland, like Scotland, has no system of archive or record storage at local level.

Until 1979 there was one single local archivist in the whole of Ireland and he was based in Cork. Then, that year, a second archivist was appointed for Dublin City and County, followed by a third for the Mid-West Counties of Limerick, Clare and North Tipperary. Since then, however, no more archivists have been appointed.

County libraries do exist, but they do not have sufficient numbers of trained staff, or materials to deal with queries, the result being that the staff there are neither enthusiastic nor over-efficient in many cases where family history research is concerned.

However, the face of Irish family history research is changing for the better. A National Genealogical Project has been launched with the intention of using a network of County Heritage Centres to computerize all Irish church registers, the 1901 Census Returns and the Tithe and Griffith's records. This project, which should be completed by 1992, will involve some 17 million entries and need computer storage of 2,000 megabytes. Enquiries should be addressed to:

Michael Byrne,
Convent View,
Tullamore,
Co. Offaly.

Today, at the end of the 1980s, the best-researched of the Republican counties have indexing projects nearing completion, namely Clare, Limerick, Offaly and Leitrim, with work going on in the remaining counties, much of it carried out in Local Heritage Centres. Some Centres are already putting their findings straight onto computer, while others have indexes made up and are considering computerization. The level of completion varies however, from county to county.

In the more advanced, such as Limerick where the archivist in charge of Mid-West Archives, Dr O'Mahony, has persuaded the bishop to allow the archives to receive copies of all indexes completed, great things may be expected. Limerick now possesses both Roman Catholic and Church of Ireland record indexes, plus copies of Methodist and Presbyterian registers which have so far not been indexed. As for Tipperary, the northern part of which is also covered by the archives, the indexing is, by contrast, nowhere near completed and, even when finished, will remain with only half its parishes under the control of the archivist. On the whole, the five years 1988 to 1993 should see the completion of the vast majority of indexing projects.

As regards Northern Ireland, Londonderry's Inner City Trust deserves a mention for its achievements in the fields of copying, transcription and publication. Founded by the Government as a job creation scheme, the Trust restores old buildings lying within the seventeenth-century Derry city walls. It employs Brian Mitchell, noted writer on Irish history and genealogy and author of several books on Irish family history already mentioned, who has established a genealogy centre. This he runs with a staff of 23 part-time researchers and two full-time supervisors.

Not only is the Centre engaged in putting the Tithe Applotment Books and Griffith's Valuation for the nine Ulster counties onto computer, it also publishes the results of its labours. With regard to the above-mentioned surveys, the Centre points out their value as they constitute in many cases the last official mention of a great many immigrants, even though only the heads of households are listed.

Apart from those books produced in association with the Genealogical Publishing Company of Baltimore, which appear in the text and in the Bibliography of this book, the Centre's publications include *A Pocket Guide to Irish Genealogy*, and parish maps of Ireland showing all townlands in Armagh, Donegal, Londonderry and Tyrone, some 6,996 in all. Also available are townland maps on microfiche for 16 counties, showing all the civil parishes. These counties are: Antrim, Armagh, Cavan, Donegal, Down, Fermanagh, Londonderry, Monaghan, Tyrone, Galway, Leitrim, Mayo, Roscommon, Sligo, Clare and Waterford. The fiches may be purchased either by county, or in sets.

Naturally enough the Genealogy Centre has concentrated its efforts initially on Co. Derry and its neighbour, Co. Donegal and records already indexed as at summer 1989 include:

Tithe Books for Co. Derry (21,277 names)
1831 Census for Co. Derry (38,651 names)
Griffith's Valuation for Co. Derry (30,715 names)
Tithe Books for Co. Donegal (28,964 names)
Griffith's Valuation for Co. Donegal (38,700 names)

Work is in hand for the indexing of both Tithe Books and Valuations for Co. Tyrone. Information has also been extracted from J. and J. Cooke's Shipping Lists 1847–1867 of emigrants leaving Derry for North America, as mentioned in Chapter Two.

The Genealogy Centre offers a research service. On receipt of 3 International Reply Coupons for a reply by airmail, the staff will search records and indexes for a fee which will depend on the nature of the enquiry. The Inner City Trust may be contacted at 10 Bishop Street, Londonderry BT48 6PW, Northern Ireland, telephone (0504) 268891; the Genealogy Centre and Heritage Library at 14 Bishop Street, telephone (0504) 269792.

A similar project, this time one which is indexing and computerizing all Roman Catholic parish registers for the

170

Archdiocese of Armagh, is that run by Father Clyne, Ara Coeli, Armagh BT61 7QY.

Finally, researchers should bear in mind that family history research is very much a changing and developing field. New discoveries, techniques and achievements are announced each year. No list, however recently or painstakingly compiled, can ever be completely up-to-date. If what you need is not immediately evident, although you are reasonably certain that it exists somewhere, have patience and do not give up too soon. Try every avenue, make all the contacts that you can, be proud of your Irish heritage and above all enjoy your research.

GLOSSARY

Anglican Communion (Churches of the): the Churches of England and Ireland, the Episcopal Church in Scotland and the Church in Wales

Anna Livia Plurabelle: James Joyce's name for the River Liffey, sometimes found as 'Anna Liffey' in songs, etc.

Báile/Bally: town or other settlement, as part of a place name.

Bann Book: a book kept in some parishes to record separately the calling of banns. In other parishes banns are entered in the parish register itself.

Blackmen: an Ulster Loyalist association.

B.M.D.: Baptisms (or Births) Marriages and Deaths.

Calendar: a list of documents, with a summary of the contents of each.

Cathedral: an Irish church; it may be a small one.

Céad Míle Fáilte: a hundred thousand welcomes.

Céilídh: an informal gathering for singing, dancing and other entertainment.

Chapel: a Catholic church in Ireland.

C.I.E.: the Irish state transport system (Córas Iompair Éireann)

Civil Registration: the compulsory state registration of births, marriages and deaths.

C.M.B.: Christenings, Marriages and Burials.

C. of E.: Church of England.

C. of I.: Church of Ireland.

Crack (the): conversation, entertainment – and much more!

Dáil Éireann: the Irish Parliament in Dublin.

Demesne: an Irish manor-house and its surrounding land.

Donagh: a large church.

Ecclesiastical Provinces: areas under the jurisdiction of an Archbishop.

Éire/Erin: Ireland; often used in a poetic or historical way.

Established Church: the denomination which is the official and therefore privileged church in a country.

Fenians: formerly, a revolutionary organization founded last

172

century in the United States in order to fight for Irish independence.

F.F.H.S.: the Federation of Family History Societies.

Filius/Filia Populi: son or daughter of the people, that is illegitimate.

Gaelic: the Irish (or Scottish) language; Irish football or coffee with whiskey.

Gaeltacht(ai): Gaelic-speaking area(s)

Garda(i): Irish policeman (men)

Golden Pages: the classified telephone directory in Ireland.

Gombeen: an exploiter, usurer or collaborator.

Green White and Orange: the Irish flag, the colours of which represent the different elements which make up the Republic.

Gregorian Calendar: the revision, by Pope Gregory XIII, in 1582, of the Julian Calendar; this was not adopted in Britain until 1752.

Incumbent: a clergyman holding a benefice.

Invincibles: an extremist rebel secret society which was responsible for the Phoenix Park Murders of the Chief and Under Secretaries for Ireland in 1882.

I.R.A.: the Irish Republican Army, a militant organisation made up of Irish nationalists aiming for a united Ireland, achieved by means of guerilla warfare. Not to be confused with the standing Army of the Irish Republic.

Irish: Irish, as opposed to Scotch, whiskey.

Julian Calendar: the one introduced by Julius Caesar in 46 BC and subsequently replaced by the Gregorian Calendar (q.v.)

Kick (or Dig) with the Other Foot: to be of the opposite religious persuasion.

King's County: former name for Offaly, the King in question being Philip II of Spain

Liberties: historically, a working-class area of Dublin; in the Middle Ages it lay outside the jurisdiction of the city authorities.

Lough: loch or lake.

MSS: manuscripts.

New/Old Style: referring to the calendar change of 1752 when Britain and America came into line with the rest of Europe by adopting the Gregorian Calendar, and the dating systems used before and after this event.

Orangemen: members of the Orange Order, so named from the Protestant King William of Orange who routed the Catholic James II at the Battle of the Boyne in 1690.

P.C.A., P.C.C., P.C.Y.: the Prerogative Courts of Armagh, Canterbury and York respectively.

Plantation: officially-sponsored settlement in Ireland by Protestant Scots or English at the expense of the Catholic Irish.

Poteen: illicitly distilled whiskey.

Praties: potatoes.

P.R.O.: Public Record Office; the Irish one has been restyled *The National Archives* since 1986.

Proddie: a Protestant.

Punt: the Irish pound.

Quarter Sessions: a criminal court held four times a year, empowered to try all but the most serious offences and to hear appeals from petty sessions.

Queen's County: former name of Co. Laois, from Mary Tudor.

Recusant: in the sixteenth to eighteenth centuries, a person who refused to attend Anglican services, thus breaking the law of the land.

Regnal Years: the years of a sovereign's reign, starting with the year of accession and ending with that of death.

Relict: the survivor of a married couple after one of the partners has died.

R.T.E.: the Irish state broadcasting company, Radio Teilifís Éireann.

Scalpeen: a hole or burrow dug into the ground and covered with branches to form a home for the destitute.

Sheriff Court: in Scotland, a court which has the power to try all but the most serious crimes and to deal with most civil actions.

Sinn Fein: 'we ourselves', a Republican political movement linked with the I.R.A. (q.v.)

Six Counties: those still forming part of Great Britain, namely: Antrim, Armagh, Derry, Down, Fermanagh and Tyrone.

Sláinte!: Cheers! (literally 'health!')

Smoke Silver: another name for Hearth Tax.

Spurious: illegitimate.

Stake: in the Mormon Church, an administrative district made up of a group of wards.

Strays: persons appearing in records of a county or parish other than that of their normal residence.

Strong Farmer: one who is not a tenant.

Taig: an impolite Ulster name for a Catholic; from the Christian name, once common in Ireland, but now replaced by 'Mick' or 'Paddy' in British usage.

Taoiseach (Taoisigh): Prime Minister(s) of the Republic.

T.D.: Member of the Irish Parliament (Teachta Dala).

Temple: a Mormon church.

Tír na n'Óg: in Irish legend the Land of Eternal Youth.

Troubles: a euphemism for the civil and religious disturbances which have torn Ireland apart this century.

TSS: typescripts.

Vid.: viduus or vidua; widower or, more frequently, widow.

Wild Geese: Irish expatriates who became professional soldiers with the Catholic powers of Europe, especially France, in the late seventeenth to early twentieth centuries.

Z: sometimes used instead of 'B', for Burials, in order to avoid confusions with Baptisms.

USEFUL ADDRESSES

The Republic of Ireland

Dublin
Dublin City Archives,
City Hall,
Dublin 2
(Telephone (01) 77 68 11)

Dublin Family History
  Society,
36 College Drive,
Templeogue,
Dublin 6

Genealogical Office,
Kildare Street,
Dublin 2
(Telephone (01) 76 55 21)

General Registrar's Office,
Joyce House,
8–11 Lombard Street East,
Dublin 2
(Telephone (01) 71 10 00)

Hibernian Research Company
  Ltd.,
Windsor House,
22 Windsor Road,
Rathmines,
Dublin 6
(Telephone (01) 96 65 22)

Irish Tourist Board (Bord
  Fáilte)
14 Upper O'Connell Street,
Dublin 1
(Telephone (01) 74 77 33)

Marsh's Library,
St Patrick's Close,
Dublin 8
(Telephone (01) 75 39 17)

National Library of Ireland,
Kildare Street,
Dublin 2
(Telephone (01) 76 55 21)

Public Record Office of
  Ireland, (*now* The National
  Archives)
Four Courts,
Dublin 1
(Telephone (01) 73 38 33)

Registry of Deeds,
Henrietta Street,
Dublin 1
(Telephone (01) 74 89 11)

Representative Church Body
  Library (RCBL)
Braemor Park,
Dublin 14
(Telephone (01) 97 99 79)

Society of Friends' Library
(Quakers)
6 Eustace Street,
Dublin 2
(Telephone (01) 77 80 88)

State Paper Office,
Birmingham Tower,
The Castle,
Dublin 2
(Telephone (01) 79 27 77)

The Provinces
Clare Heritage Centre,
Corofin,
Co. Clare
(Telephone (065) 27 632)

Cork (West) Heritage Centre,
Bandon,
Cork

Federation of Local History
Societies,
(Chairman: Very Rev. Father
Seán O'Doherty),
St Luke's Hospital,
Kilkenny
Note: s.a.e. or International
Reply Coupons essential

Irish Family History Society,
(Miss P. McCarthy,
Archivist),
Cork Archives Institute,
Christ Church,
South Main Street,
Cork
(Telephone (021) 50 90 12)
Note: may undertake research
for a fee. Annual journal
Irish Family History.

Galway County Family
History Society,
46 Maunsells Park,
Galway City

Galway-Mayo Family
Research Society,
Family Research and Heritage
Centre,
Crossboyne,
Co. Mayo

Mid-West Archives,
104 Henry Street,
Limerick
(Telephone (061) 31901)

Nenagh District Heritage
Society,
The Heritage Centre,
Nenagh,
Tipperary

Offaly Historical Society,
Charleville Road,
Tullamore,
Co. Offaly

Sligo Family History Research
Centre,
The Columban Club,
Castle Street,
Sligo
(Telephone (071) 43728)

Strokestown Heritage Society,
County Heritage Centre,
Church Street,
Strokestown,
Co. Roscommon
(Telephone (078) 33380)

Northern Ireland

Association of Ulster
Genealogists and Record
Agents,
54 Rosscoole Park,
Belfast BT14 8JX

Belfast Linen Hall Library,
Donegall Square North,
Belfast
(Telephone (0232) 321707)

Inner City Trust Genealogy
Centre,
10 Bishop Street,
Londonderry BT48 6PW
(Telephone (0504) 268891

Irish Genealogical Association,
162a Kingsway,
Dunmurry,
Belfast BT17 9AD
(Telephone (0232) 629595)
Note: arranges 'heritage
holidays' for groups and
individuals.

Mormon Church,
Belfast, Ireland, Stake,
34 Summerhill Avenue,
Belfast

North of Ireland Family
History Society,
Queen's University Teachers'
Centre,
Upper Crescent,
Belfast

Northern Ireland Tourist
Board Information Office,
River House,
48 High Street,
Belfast
(Telephone (0232) 246609)

Presbyterian Historical
Society,
Room 218,
2nd Floor,
Church House,
Fisherwick Place,
Belfast BT1 6DW

Public Record Office of
Northern Ireland
66 Balmoral Avenue,
Belfast BT9 6NY
(Telephone (0232) 6616210)

Registrar-General of Northern
Ireland,
Oxford House,
49–55 Chichester Street,
Belfast BT1 4HL
(Telephone (0232) 235211)

Scotch-Irish Trust of Ulster,
Camphill,
Omagh,
Co. Tyrone BT78 5QY
(Telephone (0662) 3292/3)

Ulster Historical Foundation,
68 Balmoral Avenue,
Belfast BT9 6NY
(Telephone (0232) 681365

Great Britain

British Library,
Reader Admissions Office,
Great Russell Street,
London WC1B 3DG
(Telephone (01) 323 7677 or
7678)
Note: the British Library is due
to move to premises near
King's Cross in the early
1990s.

Catholic Record Society,
Miss R. Rendel,
43 Lansdowne Road,
London W11 2LQ

Federation of Family History
Societies (the FFHS)
Headquarters:
The Birmingham and Midland
Institute,
Margaret Street,
Birmingham

Administrator,
Mrs Pauline Saul,
5 Mornington Close,
Copthorne,
Shrewsbury SY3 8XN

General Register Office,
St Catherine's House,
10 Kingsway,
London WC2B 6JP
(Telephone (01) 242 0262)

General Register Office for
Scotland,
New Register House,
Edinburgh EH1 3YT
(Telephone (031) 556 3952)

Irish Genealogical Research
Society,
c/o The Challoner Club,
59–61 Pont Street,
London SW1 0BD
Note: the Society's library is
open to members on
Saturday afternoons (except
on Bank Holiday weekends)
and non-members may visit
on payment of a fee.

Irish Genealogical Society,
c/o the Hon. Secretary,
5 Meredyth Road,
Barnes,
London SW12 0DS

Irish Tourist Board (Bord
Fáilte)
150 New Bond Street,
London W1Y 0AQ
(Telephone (01) 493 3201)

Liverpool City Libraries,
Record Office and Local
History Department,
William Brown Street,
Liverpool L3 8EW
(Telephone (051) 207 2147)
Note: Reader's Ticket
required; appointment
essential.

London Family History
   Centre,
64–68 Princes Gate,
Exhibition Road,
London SW7 2PA
(Telephone (01) 589 8561)

National Library of Scotland,
George IV Bridge,
Edinburgh EH
(Telephone (031) 226 453)

National Library of Wales,
Department of Manuscripts
   and Records,
Aberystwyth,
·Dyfed SY23 3BU
(Telephone (0970) 3816/7)
Note: Admission by Reader's
   Ticket; written application
   only.

Northern Irish Tourist Board,
11 Berkeley Street,
London W1X
(Telephone (01) 493 0601)

Principal Probate Registry,
Somerset House,
Strand,
London WC2R 1LA
(Telephone (01) 405 7641)

Public Record Office,
Chancery Lane,
London WC2A 1LR
(Telephone (01) 405 0741)
Note: Reader's Ticket
   required. Closed for stock-
   taking first full two weeks
   in October.

Public Record Office,
Ruskin Avenue,
Kew,
Richmond,
Surrey TW9 4DU
(Telephone (01) 876 3444)
Admission as above.

Public Record Office,
Land Registry Building
(for Censuses)
Portugal Street,
London WC2A 1LR
(Telephone (01) 405 3488)
Note: Day Pass issued at door
   unless Reader's Ticket held.
   No advance bookings
   accepted.

Scottish Record Office,
PO Box 36,
H.M. General Register House,
Edinburgh EH1 3YT
(Telephone (031) 556 6585 and
   557 1022)

Society of Genealogists'
   Library,
14 Charterhouse Buildings,
London EC1M 7BA
(Telephone (01) 8790/8799)

Australia

National Library of Australia,
Parkes Place,
Canberra ACT 2600
(Telephone (062) 61 1111)

Australian National
   University Library,
Canberra ACT 2602

State Library of New South
Wales (*including the Mitchell
Library*)
Maquarie Street,
Sydney NSW 2000
(Telephone (02) 221 1388)

Archives Office of New South
Wales,
2 Globe Street,
Sydney NWS 2000
(Telephone (02) 237 0152)

Northern Territory Archives
Service,
Corner McMinn and Kerry
Streets,
Darwin NT 5790
(Telephone (089) 82 1261)

Archives Office of
Queensland,
162 Annerley Road,
Dutton Park Qld. 4102
(Telephone (07) 443 215)
Note: No queries answered by
either mail or telephone.

State Library of South
Australia,
Archives Department,
North Terrace,
Adelaide SA 5000
(Telephone (08) 223 8911)

State Library of Tasmania,
Archives Department,
91 Murray Street,
Hobart Tas. 7000
(Telephone (002) 30 8033)

State Library of Victoria,
Archives Division,
304–324 Swanston Street,
Melbourne Vic. 3000
(Telephone (03) 669 9888)

State Library of Western
Australia,
Archives Branch,
Alexander Library Building,
Perth Cultural Centre,
James Street,
Perth WA 6000
(Telephone (09) 328 7466)

Civil Registration

New South Wales:
The Registrar General,
Prince Albert Road,
Sydney NSW 2000
(Telephone (02) 228 6666

Northern Territory:
The Registrar General,
PO Box 3021,
Darwin NT 5794
(Telephone (089) 89 8911)

Queensland:
The Registrar General's
Office,
Old Treasury Buildings,
Queen Street,
Brisbane Qld. 4000
(Telephone (07) 224 0616)

South Australia:
The Registrar General,
Principal Registry Office,
Edmund Wright House,
59 King William Street,
Adelaide SA 5000
(Telephone (08) 227 3699)

Tasmania:
Registrar General's Division,
Births, Deaths and
Marriages,
Law Department,
81 Murray Street,
Hobart Tas. 7000
(Telephone (002) 30 8011)

Victoria:
Registrar General's Office,
Law Department,
233 William Street,
Melbourne Vic. 3000
(Telephone (03) 602 2200)

Western Australia:
The Registrar General,
Oakleigh Building,
22 St George's Terrace,
Perth WA 6000
(Telephone (09) 325 5799)

Some leading genealogical societies

Australian Institute of
Genealogical Studies,
PO Box 68,
Oakleigh Vic. 3166

Heraldry and Genealogy
Society of Canberra,
GPO Box 585,
Canberra ACT 2601

Society of Australian
Genealogists,
Richmond Villa,
120 Kent Street,
Observatory Hill,
Sydney NSW 2000

Genealogical Society of
Northern Territory,
PO Box 37212,
Winnellie NT 5789

Genealogical Society of
Queensland,
PO Box 423,
Woolloongabba Qld 4012

Southern Australian
Genealogical and Heraldry
Society,
GPO Box 592,
Adelaide SA 5001

Genealogical Society of
Tasmania,
PO Box 640G,
Hobart Tas 7001

Genealogical Society of
Victoria,
5th Floor,
Curtin House,
252 Swanston Street,
Melbourne Vic 3000

Western Australian
Genealogical Society,
5/48 May Street,
Bayswater WA 6053

New Zealand

National Archives of New
Zealand,
PO Box 6162,
Te Aro,
Wellington

Registrar-General,
Registry of Births, Deaths and
  Marriages,
Levin House,
Private Bag,
Lower Hutt,
Wellington

Genealogical Research
  Institute of New Zealand
  Inc.,
PO Box 36107,
Moera,
Lower Hutt,
Wellington

New Zealand Federation of
  Family History Societies,
Mrs J. Lord,
PO Box 13301,
Armagh,
Christchurch

New Zealand Society of
  Genealogists Inc.,
PO Box 8795,
Auckland 3
Note: see also Australian
  sections, in particular New
  South Wales and Tasmania,
  as New Zealand was first
  governed from Sydney,
  where many early arrivals
  disembarked prior to
  moving on to New
  Zealand. See also archive
  material for both Australia
  and New Zealand in Great
  Britain and Ireland.

Canada

National and Provincial Archives

Public Archives of Canada,
395 Wellington Street,
Ottawa
ON K1A ON3
(Telephone (613) 995–5138)

Provincial Archives of
  Alberta,
12845–102nd Avenue,
Edmonton
AB T5N OM6
(Telephone (403) 427–1750)

Provincial Archives of British
  Columbia,
Parliament Buildings,
655 Belleville Street,
Victoria
BC V8V IX4
(Telephone (604) 387–5885)

Provincial Archives of
  Manitoba,
200 Vaughan Street,
Winnipeg
MB R3C 0PB
(Telephone (204) 944–3971)

Provincial Archives of New
  Brunswick,
PO Box 6000,
Fredericton
NB E3B 5HI
(Telephone (506) 453–2637)

Provincial Archives of
Newfoundland and
Labrador,
Colonial Building,
Military Road,
St John's
NF A1C 2C9
(Telephone (709) 753–9390)

Archives of the Northwest
Territories,
Prince of Wales Northern
Heritage Centre,
Yellowknife,
NWT X1A 2L9
(Telephone (403) 873–7698)

Provincial Archives of Nova
Scotia,
6016 University Avenue,
Halifax
NS B3H IW4
(Telephone (902) 423–9115)

Provincial Archives of
Ontario,
77 Grenville Street,
Queen's Park,
Toronto
ON M7A 2R9
(Telephone (416) 965–4030)

Public Archives of Prince
Edward Island,
Coles Building,
Richmond Street,
Charlottetown
PEI C1A 7M4
(Telephone (902) 892–7949)

Archives Nationales du
Québec,
1210 ave du Séminaire,
CP 10450
Sainte-Foy,
PQ G1V 4N1
(Telephone (418) 643–2167)

Saskatchewan Archives Board,
Regina Office,
Library Building,
University of Regina,
Regina
SK S4S 0A2
Telephone (306) 565–4068)

Saskatchewan Archives Board,
Saskatoon Office,
Murray Memorial Building,
University of Saskatchewan,
Saskatoon,
SK S7N OWO
(Telephone (306) 664–5832)

Yukon Archives (also the
address of the Registrar
General)
PO Box 2703
Whitehorse,
YT Y1A 2C6
(Telephone (403) 667–5321)

Some leading genealogical societies

Alberta Genealogical Society,
Box 12015,
Edmonton,
Alberta T5J 3L2

British Columbia Genealogical
  Society,
Box 94371,
Richmond,
BC V6Y 2A8

Manitoba Genealogical
  Society,
420–167 Lombard Avenue,
Winnipeg,
Manitoba R3B 0T6

New Brunswick Genealogical
  Society,
PO Box 3235,
Station B,
Fredericton,
NB E3A 5G9

Genealogical Association of
  Nova Scotia,
PO Box 895,
Armdale,
NS B3L 4K5

Ontario Genealogical Society,
Ste 253,
40 Orchard View Boulevard,
Toronto
ON M4R 1B9

Prince Edward Island
  Genealogical Society,
Box 2744,
Charlottetown,
PE1 C1A 8C4

Quebec Family History
  Society,
164 Lakeshore Road,
Pointe Claire,
Quebec H9S 4J9

Saskatchewan Genealogical
  Society,
1870 Lorne Street,
Regina,
SK S4P 2L7

United States of America

Ancestry Inc.,
PO Box 476,
Salt Lake City,
Utah 84110

Board for the Certification of
  Genealogists,
1307 New Hampshire Avenue
  N.W.,
Washington DC 20036
Note: the Board will put
  enquirers in touch with
  accredited genealogists
  willing to trace emigrant
  ancestors for a fee.

Family History Library of the
  Mormon Church
50 East North Temple,
Salt Lake City,
Utah 84150
Note: No research service as
  such.

Irish Family Names Society,
PO Box 2095,
La Mesa Ca 92041

Irish Genealogical Society,
99 Ash Street,
New Bedford Ma 02740

Irish Tourist Board Offices
(Bord Fáilte)
757 Third Avenue,
New York NY 10017

National Archives and
Records Service,
General Services
Administration,
Washington DC 20408
Note: There are countless
archives and societies at all
local levels throughout the
United States. In addition,
material held by the Public
Record Offices in London,
Dublin and Belfast should
be borne in mind.

South Africa

The Division for Biographical
and Genealogical Research,
Institute for Historical
Research,
Human Sciences Research
Council,
Pvt. Bag X41,
Pretoria 0001

The Genealogical Society of
South Africa,
PO Box 3057,
Coetzenburg 7602

The Government Archives and
Heraldic Services,
Ministry of National
Education,
Pvt. Bag X236,
Pretoria 0001

BIBLIOGRAPHY

General

Anderson Black, J., *Your Irish Ancestors*, Paddington Press, New York, 1974.

Irish Genealogist, The, annual Journal of the Irish Genealogical Research Society, London.

Mitchell, Brian, *Pocket Guide to Irish Genealogy*, Genealogical Centre, Derry.

Neill, K., *How to Trace Family History in Northern Ireland*, available from the Irish Genealogical Association, Belfast.

O'Hart, J., *Irish Pedigrees*, 2 volumes, reprint of the 5th edition, Dublin, 1892, by the Genealogical Publishing Company, Inc. Baltimore, 1989.

Ryan, J., *Irish Records: Sources for Family and Local History*, Ancestry Inc., Salt Lake City.

Songs Most Popular in Ireland (3 volumes), Ossian Books, Cork, 1979.

Chapter 1: Setting the scene, pp. 1–27

Cassell's Illustrated History of England, Limited Subscribers' Edition, no date, *c.* 1908.

General Alphabetical Index to the Townlands and Towns, Parishes and Baronies of Ireland. Based on the census of Ireland for the Year 1851. Edition of 1861 reissued by the Genealogical Publishing Co. Inc., Baltimore, 1986.

Irish Department of Foreign Affairs, *Facts About Ireland*, Dublin, 1981.

Mitchell, B., *A New Genealogical Atlas of Ireland*, Genealogical Publishing Co. Inc. Baltimore, 1986.

O'Brien, M. and C. C., *A Concise History of Ireland*, Thames and Hudson, London, 1985

Public Record Office of Ireland (now the National Archives)

Study Packs from facsimile documents:
1. *The Rebellion of 1798*
2. *The Famine – Ireland 1845–51*
Wells, J. C., *Accents of English: 2. The British Isles*, Cambridge University Press, 1982.
Woodham-Smith, C., *The Great Hunger*, New English Library, London 1963.

Chapter 2: The Leaving of Ireland, pp. 28–42

Coldham, P. W., *The Complete Book of Emigrants 1607–1660*, Genealogical Publishing Co. Inc., Baltimore, 1987.
Crick, B. and Alman, M., *A Guide to Manuscripts Relating to America in Great Britain and Ireland*, British Association for American Studies, revised edition, Oxford, 1979.
Famine Immigrants, The, Lists of Irish Immigrants Arriving at the Port of New York 1846–1851, in 7 volumes, Genealogical Publishing Co., Inc., Baltimore, 1983–1986.
Merseyside Maritime Museum, *Emigration Packs: UK and Eire* and *USA and Canada*, and *Australia and New Zealand*, National Museums and Galleries on Merseyside, Liverpool.
Merseyside Maritime Museum, *Emigrants to a New World*, Exhibition Souvenir Booklet, National Museums and Galleries on Merseyside, Liverpool.
Mitchell, Brian, *Irish Emigration Lists 1833–1839*, Lists of Emigrants Extracted from the Ordnance Survey Memoirs of Counties Londonderry and Antrim. Genealogical Publishing Co. Inc. Baltimore 1989.
Mitchell, Brian, *Irish Passenger Lists 1847–1871*. Lists of Passengers Sailing from Londonderry to America on Ships of the J. and J. Cooke Line and the McCorkell Line. Genealogical Publishing Co. Inc., Baltimore, 1988.
Schlegel, D. M. *Passengers from Ireland*. Lists of Passengers Arriving at American Ports Between 1811 and 1817. Transcribed from the *Shamrock* or *Hibernian Chronicle*. Genealogical Publishing Co. Inc., Baltimore, 1980.

Chapter 3: Making a Start with Research, pp. 43–54

Public Record Office of Ireland (now The National Archives), *The National School System 1831–1924*.

Tully Cross Guild of the Irish Countrywomen's Association, *Portrait of a Parish, Ballynakill, Connemara*, 1985.

Chapter 4: The Ancestor Abroad: The British Mainland, pp. 55–80

Cox, J. and Padfield, T., *Tracing Your Ancestors in the Public Record Office*, PRO Handbook No. 19, HMSO, 1984.

Family Tree Magazine, 141 Great Whyte, Ramsey, Huntingdon, Cambridgeshire, PE17 1HP. Published monthly.

Gibson, J. S. W., *Census Returns 1841–1881 on Microfilm: A Directory of Local Holdings*, Federation of Family History Societies, 4th edition, 1986 (5th edition in preparation).

Gibson, J. S. W. and West, J., *Local Newspapers Before 1920 in England, Wales and the Isle of Man: A Select List*, FFHS, 1987.

Gibson, J. S. W. and Peskett, P., *Record Offices: How to Find Them*, FFHS, 4th edition, 1987.

Gibson, J. S. W., *General Register Offices and the I.G.I.: Where to Find Them*, FFHS, 1987.

Gibson, J. S. W., *Wills and Where to Find Them*, Phillimore, 1974.

Richardson, J., *The Local Historian's Encyclopaedia*, Historical Publications, New Barnet, 1986.

Rogers, C., *The Family Tree Detective*, Manchester University Press, 1986.

Thompson, Flora, *Lark Rise to Candleford*, The World's Classics, Oxford University Press, 1971.

Williams, J. Anthony, *Sources for Recusant History (1559–1791) in English Official Archives*, Catholic Record Society journal *Recusant History*, Volume 16, Number 4 (October 1983).

Chapter 5: The Ancestor Abroad: The New World, pp. 81–106

Adams, W. F., *Ireland and Irish Emigration to the New World. From 1815 to the Famine*, reprint of the 1932 edition, Genealogical Publishing Co. Inc., Baltimore, 1980.

Baxter, A., *In Search of Your British and Irish Roots*, Macmillan, Toronto, 1989.

Baxter, A., *In Search of Your Canadian Roots*, Genealogical Publishing Co. Inc., Baltimore, 1989.

Coleman, T., *Going to America*, 1972, reprinted 1987, Genealogical Publishing Co. Inc., Baltimore.

Eakle, A. and Cerny, J. (eds.), *The Source*, Ancestry Publishing Co., Salt Lake City, 1984.

Hall, Nick Vine, *Tracing Your Family History in Australia*, Rigby, 1985.

McCracken, D. P. *The Irish Pro-Boers*, Perskor Books, Johannesburg, 1989.

Tepper, M., *American Passenger Arrival Records*, Genealogical Publishing Co. Inc., Baltimore, 1988.

Chapters 6 and 7: The Ancestor at Home; Interpreting the Records, pp. 107–153

Begley, D. F., *The Ancestor Trail in Ireland*, Heraldic Artists, Dublin, 1982.

Begley, D. F., *Handbook on Irish Genealogy*, Heraldic Artists, Dublin, 1983.

Begley, D. F., *Irish Genealogy: A Record Finder*, Heraldic Artists, Dublin, 1981

Falley, M. D., *Irish and Scotch-Irish Ancestral Research: a Guide to Genealogical Records, Methods and Sources in Ireland*, 2 volumes, first edition of 1962 reissued by the Genealogical Publishing Co. Inc., Baltimore, 1988.

Griffith, M., *A Short Guide to the Public Record Office of Ireland*, Dublin, 1964.

Irish Genealogical Research Association, *A Simple Guide to Irish Genealogy*, London, 1966.

Mitchell, Brian, *A Guide to Irish Parish Registers*, Genealogical Publishing Co. Inc., Baltimore, 1988.

Return of Owners of Land in Ireland 1876, reprinted by the Genealogical Publishing Co. Inc., Baltimore, 1988.

Public Record Office of Ireland (National Archives), *The Public Record Office – Sources for Local Studies in the Public Record Office of Ireland*.

Vicars, Sir Arthur, *Index to the Prerogative Wills of Ireland 1536–1810*. Original edition of 1897 reissued by the Genealogical Publishing Co. Inc., Baltimore, 1989.

Chapter 8: Visiting Ireland, pp. 154–171

British Overseas Trade Board, *Hints to Exporters: The Republic of Ireland*.

Fodor's Modern Guides, *Ireland*, New York, 1988.

Insight Guides, *Ireland*, APA Productions (Hong Kong) Ltd., 1986.

Irish Department of Foreign Affairs, *Facts About Ireland*, Dublin, 1981.

Irish Tourist Board Annual Brochure, Maps and Booklets.

Northern Ireland Tourist Board Annual Brochure, Maps and Booklets.

INDEX